Automotive Electronic Systems

TREVOR MELLARD

HEINEMANN : LONDON

William Heinemann Ltd
10 Upper Grosvenor Street, London W1X 9PA

LONDON   MELBOURNE   JOHANNESBURG   AUCKLAND

First published 1987
© William Heinemann Ltd 1987

British Library Cataloguing in Publication Data
Mellard, Trevor.
   Automotive electronic systems.
   1. Motor vehicles – Electronic equipment
   I. Title
   629.2'7   TL272.5

ISBN 0 434 91257 3

Printed and bound in Great Britain by
Robert Hartnoll (1985) Ltd., Bodmin, Cornwall

0865 - 311 - 3666

Contents

Preface

Progress in the application of electronics to the automobile has been rapid, and the next era will bring many more developments. To rise to the challenge offered, the service technician needs an understanding of electronic principles, technology and practices. The book is designed to give an outline of the technological principles and practices used in modern electronic automotive systems. The inner workings of the electronic control units are included to enhance the reader's comprehension of electronic systems, but at no point should readers feel that they are getting out of their depth.

The descriptions and explanations are clear and precise and are further consolidated by the extensive use of illustrations alongside the written material.

The diagrams, drawings and illustrations are used to help explain theoretical principles and are in no way intended to be a design base for practical working circuits.

The design base for the book assumes that the reader will have an understanding of basic electrical, electronic and microelectronic principles, or will have accesss to the many textbooks available covering this level of the subject.

The book seeks to build upon this and provide updating information and knowledge for experienced electronics people as well as the automobile technician and student.

Acknowledgements

The author is grateful and wishes to acknowledge the valuable assistance received in the preparation of this book to the following; for their permission to reproduce illustrations, and for help in providing material:

AB Electronics Products Group Prof. D.M. Embry
C. ENG. F.J. OP Der Winkel
Austin Rover Group Limited
Armstrong Patents Co. Limited
Robert Bosch Limited
Ford Motor Company
Vauxhall Motors Limited
Lucas Electrical Limited
Nissan Motor Company Limited
Toyota Motor Company Limited

Society of Automotive Engineers
Association of Motor Vehicle Teachers
Society of Auto-Electrical Technicians
The Institute of Electrical and Electronic Engineers
Lotus Car Company Limited
VAG (UK) Limited

Every effort has been made to identify and reach copyright holders; much of the material is drawn from past experiences and the reading of vast amounts of information for the preparation of education and training programmes. If I have unwittingly infringed any copyright, I apologise and would be grateful to hear from any such source.

Introduction

Although automotive electronics has only recently come into the limelight, the relationship between motor vehicles and electronic technology dates back more than half a century.

Today, electronic devices are controlled either by analogue or by digital systems, but the trend is towards the exclusive use of digital. Eventually every computer system in the car may well be linked together, providing fully integrated control of the entire vehicle and outstanding improvement in function and reliability.

Automotive electronic equipment comes in various shapes and forms ranging from small signalling devices housing transistors and diodes, to fully fledged computers with microprocessors, IC memories and input/output interfaces. To date, electronics has been used in a wide variety of applications including the engine, transmission, brakes, driving operators, power sources, instrument panel displays, air conditioning and radios.

This integration of electronics and the automobile makes possible control capabilities far beyond those realised through mechanical technology: the result being dramatic improvements in all phases of automotive function, from driving performance to fuel efficiency, exhaust purification, safety and comfort. No doubt, too, that electronics will find many more applications in an ever wider variety of automotive fields.

The rapid application of electronics to automotive technology has also created problems for the industry's service personnel. Students, technicians, managers, teachers and car owners are often bewildered by the sight and operation of automotive electronic systems, and many do not feel confident in servicing, repairing and fault diagnosing them. Therefore the need exists for a wide variety of persons, in particular service technicians and engineers, to be fully versed in the operating principles, skills, knowledge and abilities required to fault diagnose and repair automotive electronic systems – thus providing the car-owning public with well trained, educated and quick-thinking service technicians, capable of providing good service and quality repairs.

There is little available in the way of educational material at the moment. This book seeks to rectify this and meet the objectives outlined above by providing the much needed information in a clear precise manner.

The book will be of benefit to students on a variety of City and Guilds and BTEC technician courses. It will serve also as an ideal reference text for qualified craftsmen, technicians and engineers who wish to keep their skills and knowledge up to date, or for whom it is mandatory to have a working knowledge of automotive electronics.

Automotive electronics is here to stay, it is the only way to control today's car and the car of the future. It is essential to all concerned with motor vehicle engineering to keep up with the latest – and future – developments. This book provides that opportunity and much more.

About the author

Trevor Mellard teaches automotive electronics at West Glamorgan Institute of Higher Education, Swansea, where he is Head of the School of Automobile Engineering. Mr Mellard has taught courses in automotive electrical and electronics at both FE and advanced FE levels. As a member of both City and Guilds and BTEC working parties and committees he has written education and training material, designed electrical and electronic curricula and learning modules. At present he is a City and Guilds examiner in electrical and electronic work, and an advisor to BTEC in the same subject areas. Professionally he is a Member of the Chartered Institute of Transport, Member of the Institute of the Motor Industry, an Associate Member of the Institute of Road Transport Engineers and a Member of the Society of Auto-Electrical Technicians. He is Honorary Secretary of a learned Society, the Association of Motor Vehicle Teachers.

1

Fundamentals of automotive technology

Electronic technology is now applied to a diverse spectrum of automobile operations; helping to improve driving performance, fuel efficiency, emissions purification, comfort and pleasure. In this chapter we consider the relevant systems of an automobile which can be controlled electronically:

1   engine
2   transmission
3   suspension
4   steering
5   brakes
6   instrumentation.

Fig 1.1 shows the layout of these systems. Following chapters discuss how electronic control of these systems can take place.

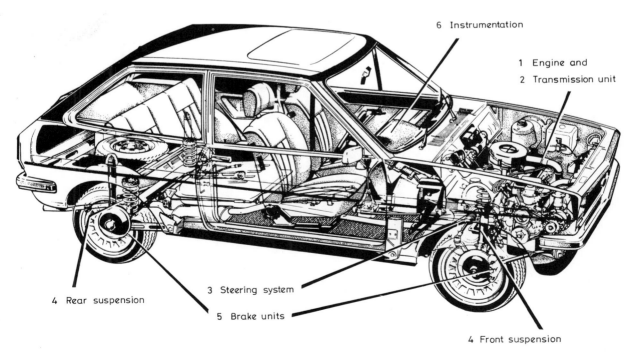

6   Instrumentation

1   Engine and
2   Transmission unit

4   Rear suspension

3   Steering system

5   Brake units

4   Front suspension

Fig 1.1   Basic automobile systems

Internal combustion engine

The engine is a self-contained power unit which converts the heat energy of fuel into mechanical energy for moving the vehicle. Because fuel is burned within, the engine is known as an internal combustion (IC) engine. In the IC engine, an air-fuel mixture is introduced into a closed cylinder where it is compressed and then ignited. The burning of the fuel (combustion) causes a rapid rise in cylinder pressure which is converted to useful mechanical energy by the piston and crankshaft.

The fuel may be ignited either by a spark or by compression giving rise to classifications of spark-

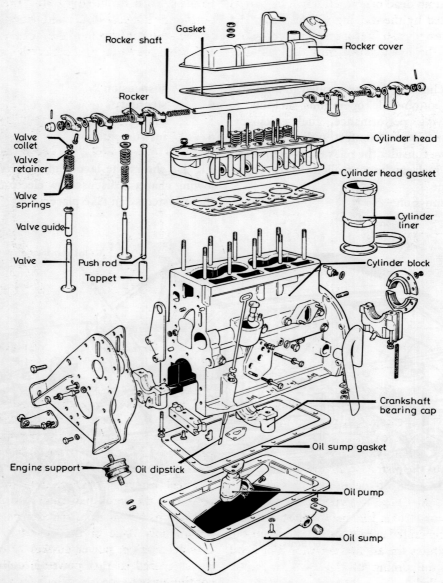

Fig 1.2   An in-line overhead valve engine – fixed parts and valve mechanism

ignition (SI) and compression-ignition (CI) engines. An exploded view of a typical spark ignition petrol engine is shown in Fig 1.2, detailing the major components.

The four strokes of such an engine are shown in Fig 1.3. At the beginning of the induction stroke Fig 1.3(a) the inlet valve opens and the piston travels down the cylinder from top dead centre (TDC) to bottom dead centre (BDC). The partial vacuum created by the moving piston causes the air-fuel mixture to rush in from the inlet manifold and through the open valve, into the cylinder.

causing a rapid and extreme rise in cylinder pressure, to such an extent that the piston is forced down the cylinder and the connecting rod gives the crankshaft a powerful turning effort. This is the combustion stroke, also called the power stroke, shown in Fig 1.3(c).

Once the mixture has been burned it must be removed from the cylinder as quickly as possible. In the exhaust stroke (Fig 1.3(d)) the rising piston pushes the hot gases and combustion products out of the cylinder through the open exhaust valve and exhaust system into the earth's atmosphere.

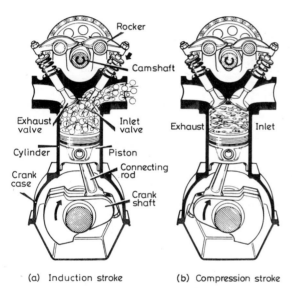
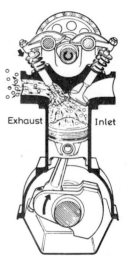

(a) Induction stroke (b) Compression stroke (c) Combustion stroke (d) Exhaust stroke

Fig 1.3 Four stroke cycle principle of operation

The correct air-fuel mixture is provided by the carburettor. When the piston reaches the end of its stroke the inlet valve closes, sealing the top end of the cylinder as both valves are closed.

In Fig 1.3(b) the piston is moving up the cylinder, compressing the air-fuel mixture between the piston and cylinder head to a very small volume – the compression stroke. Just before TDC an electrical spark, generated across the electrodes of the spark plug, ignites the air-fuel mixture. For good performance the timing of the spark must be closely controlled.

As the mixture burns, the hot gas expands

This sequence of events is repeated continually, with power delivered to the crankshaft on only one of the four strokes – the combustion stroke. Crankshaft rotation continues through the other strokes due to the kinetic energy of the heavy flywheel which is connected to the crankshaft. Note that the crankshaft rotates through *two* full revolutions for each four-stroke cycle and a spark occurs only once in the cylinder. In a multi-cylinder engine, power strokes of each cylinder are staggered so that power is delivered almost continuously to the crankshaft for a smooth operation.

Mixture supply system

Fuel stored in a large tank, is fed via a pump to the carburettor. The carburettor (Fig 1.4) mixes the liquid petrol with filtered air on its way to the

moves towards the horizontal position the airflow is restricted (throttled) and engine power and speed is reduced accordingly. In normal operation the air-fuel ratio (by mass) varies, typically, in the range 12:1 to 17:1.

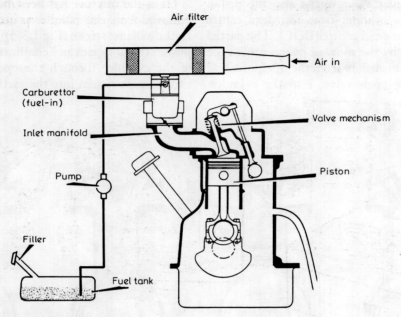

Fig 1.4   Basic fuel supply system

cylinders and in the process turns it into a vapour. The inlet manifold (Fig 1.5) directs the mixture to the cylinders. The ratio of air to fuel in the mixture delivered to the cylinder is controlled by the size and shape of the carburettor bore and venturi, and the size of the fuel metering jets. The standard manual control for the amount of air and fuel mixture delivered to the engine is the throttle valve, which is controlled by the driver's depression of the accelerator pedal. The throttle valve is simply a round disc, mounted on a thin pivot shaft so that it can be tilted at different angles under the control of the accelerator pedal. In the vertical position the throttle valve offers virtually no restriction and the full volume of air and fuel passes to the cylinders to produce maximum engine power. As the throttle valve

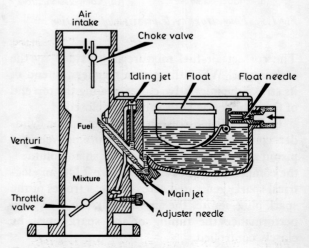

Fig 1.5   Mixture supply principles

Ignition systems

The basic ignition system of the SI petrol engine is the Kettering system (Fig 1.6). The battery provides a low voltage (12 V) source of direct current. When the ignition switch is turned on and the contact breaker points are closed (Fig 1.7(a)) current flows through the primary winding of the ignition coil. This current flow creates a magnetic field in the primary coil. When the contact breaker points open, interrupting the flow of current (Fig 1.7(b)) a rapid voltage change is produced across the primary winding and a high voltage (15,000–20,000 V) is induced across the secondary winding. This secondary voltage is high enough to jump the gap of a spark plug, creating a spark between

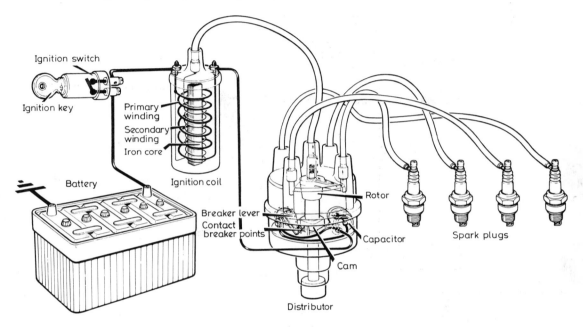

Fig 1.6   Basic Kettering ignition system used in SI petrol engines

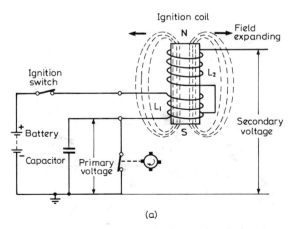
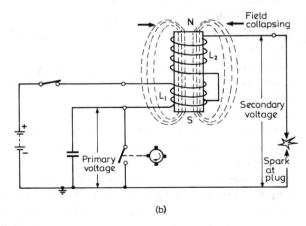

Fig 1.7   Basic Kettering ignition system principles
(a) with contact breaker points closed

(b) with contact breaker points open

the electrodes with sufficient energy and direction to ignite the air-fuel mixture. To assist in the rapid change of primary voltage a capacitor is connected in parallel with the breaker points, which also reduces arcing across the points – extending useful life.

The high voltage pulses generated across the secondary coil winding must be delivered to the appropriate spark plug at the correct time. The distributor, shown in Fig 1.6, is used for this purpose.

It contains a rotary switch (rotor) and fixed cap, that connects the secondary pulse to the appropriate spark plug just before the corresponding piston reaches TDC on the compression stroke. The distributor is connected to the coil and spark plugs by high tension plug leads and the distributor shaft controls the opening and closing of the contact breaker points. As the spark (ignition) timing must be related to the position of the piston in the cylinder the distributor shaft rotation must be coupled to the crankshaft. This coupling is made by mechanical gearing to the camshaft, which is crankshaft driven. The camshaft rotates at half the speed of the crankshaft, because only one spark and one valve sequence is required for each two revolutions of the crankshaft.

Initial ignition timing of the Kettering system is set by positioning number one cylinder piston just before TDC, both valves closed, at the end of the compression stroke. The contact breaker points are then set to just opening with the rotor feeding the number one cylinder plug lead. Prior to this, the gap between the *fully* open points must be set, to give correct dwell time.

When the engine is running, timing of the ignition spark must be controlled so that the complete charge of air-fuel mixture within a cylinder has fully combusted, or 'burned' through, at the exact moment the corresponding piston starts to go down the cylinder from TDC on the power stroke; because the full combustion power is then available and maximum useful work is produced. In this respect the fuel mixture burn time is almost constant but, two factors must be taken into consideration. First, the burn-time varies with air-fuel mixture pressure – the higher the pressure, the longer the necessary burn-time. Second, the burn-time is independent of engine speed – the faster the engine speed, the greater the angle through which its crankshaft turns during the burn.

To ensure the burn is always completed at the correct time – whatever the load conditions and engine speed – compensation adjustments must be made to advance timing of the ignition spark with: (1) increasing air-fuel mixture pressure, and; (2) increasing engine speeds. These adjustments are automatically performed in two ways:

- a device known as a vacuum advance senses the pressure of the air-fuel mixture within the inlet manifold and retards the timing as the pressure decreases (i.e. as the 'vacuum' increases). As the pressure is related to engine load it can be seen that the ignition timing retards with increasing load.
- a device known as a centrifugal advance senses engine speed and advances ignition timing as speed increases.

Ignition timing has significant effects on engine performance. Correct advance of timing provides complete combustion hence high power output and low exhaust emissions. *Too* advanced ignition timing, however, results in the combustion pressure opposing the rising piston with a resulting loss of power, high mechanical stress conditions and detonation that causes an audible pinging (knock) sound. Retarded ignition timing can result in incomplete combustion, low power output, overheating and increased exhaust emission. To balance out these conflicting features, engines are generally tuned to a static ignition timing of about 8 to 10 degrees BTDC, with the automatic advance and retard mechanisms catering for variable conditions.

Diesel engine

The diesel engine, although similar to the petrol engine in construction, is normally heavier and used mostly in heavy duty vehicles. Like the petrol engine it extracts its energy by burning an air-fuel mixture inside cylinders; the pistons, connecting rods and crankshafts are similar and the four-stroke cycle occurs in the same sequence. The main differences are in the way in which the air and fuel are introduced into the cylinders and the way in which the air-fuel mixture is ignited.

Air alone enters the cylinder on the induction stroke and is compressed by the upstroke of the piston in the compression stroke, during which time it becomes extremely hot (650°C) and pressurised (3.5MPa). Diesel fuel in the form of a spray is injected just before TDC. The fuel is self-ignited by the high temperature of the compressed air and the burning gases expand and force the piston down.

The pressure developed by the piston's compression stroke is greater than in a petrol engine – normally two to three times higher. The combustion process lasts for most of the power stroke and the resulting pressure remains approximately the same throughout the stroke.

Power and speed output of the diesel engine are controlled by the quantity of fuel injected into the cylinders, as the amount of air that enters the cylinder on each induction stroke is almost constant. The fuel is injected through an injector spray nozzle at each cylinder, supplied by a fuel injection pump. The amount of fuel injected into each charge of air is extremely small and each shot of fuel is measured with great accuracy.

Transmission

The transmission system comprises clutch, gearbox, propellor shaft, rear axle and differential and the driven road wheels.

Clutch

The clutch or torque converter has the task of disconnecting and connecting the engine's power from and to the driving wheels of the vehicle. This action may be manual or automatic.

Gearbox

The main purpose of the gearbox is to provide a selection of gear ratios between the engine and driving wheels, so that the vehicle can operate satisfactorily under all driving conditions. Gear selection may be done manually by the driver or automatically by a hydraulic control system.

Propellor shaft

The function of the propellor (drive) shaft is to transmit the drive from the gearbox to the input shaft of the rear axle and differential assembly. Flexible joints allow the rear axle and wheels to move up and down without affecting operation.

Rear axle and differential

The rear axle and differential unit transmits the engine's rotational power through 90° from propshaft to axle shaft to road wheels. A further function is to allow each driven wheel to turn at a different speed; essential when cornering because the outer wheel must turn further than the inside wheel. A third function is to introduce another gear ratio for torque multiplication.

Suspension

The axles and wheels are isolated from the chassis by a suspension system. The basic job of the suspension system is to absorb the shocks caused by irregular road surfaces that would otherwise be transmitted to the vehicle and its occupants, thus helping to keep the vehicle on a controlled and level course, regardless of road conditions.

Steering

The steering system, under the control of the driver at the steering wheel, provides the means by which the front wheels are directionally turned. The steering system may be power assisted to reduce the effort required to turn the steering wheel and make the vehicle easier to manoeuvre.

Brakes

The braking system on a vehicle has three main functions. It must be able to reduce the speed of the vehicle, when necessary; it must be able to stop the car in as short a distance as possible; it must be able to hold the vehicle stationary. The braking action is achieved as a result of the friction developed by forcing a stationary surface (the brake lining) into contact with a rotating surface (the drum or disc).

Each wheel has a brake assembly, of either the drum type or the disc type, hydraulically operated when the driver applies the foot brake pedal.

Instrumentation

The motor vehicle incorporates a number of electrical devices which are used for:

Battery charging	– alternator and regulator.
Engine purposes	– starting and ignition.
Safety and convenience	– lighting, horn, wipers, washers etc.
Driver information	– instrumentation and warning lamps.

Of these devices instrumentation is, perhaps, most influenced by the advance of micro-electronics. The basic electromechanical systems of:

Speedometer	– for indicating vehicle speed.
Engine oil pressure	– warning lamp or gauge to show operating limits.
Engine coolant temperature	– warning lamp or gauge to show operating limits.
Battery charging	– warning lamp or gauge to indicate satisfactory/ unsatisfactory action.
Fuel tank content	– gauge to show amount of fuel in the fuel tank.

are giving way to computerised vehicle management information centres.

2

Automotive electronic and microprocessor systems

A system is defined as an orderly arrangement of physical objects. It can be organised into three basic elements: input, processor and output, as shown in Fig 2.1. The input signal is usually the

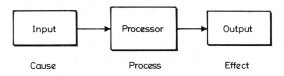

Fig 2.1   Basic idea of a system having organized inputs and outputs

cause of a change in the system and the output action which occurs as a result of the input is called the *effect*, while the response of the system to an input signal is called the *process* where the input is processed to effect the desired output. A system can be purely analogue in nature, purely digital, or a mixture of both.

Initially, a system senses external information, converting it to a form that can be handled internally. Then decisions are made, based on the input information, by process or manipulation. In mak-

ing a decision a system may store the information for a time, or process it as the result of other information stored permanently in memory. Finally, as the result of the decision, an action outside the system takes place.

This three-element system configuration is very simple. Typically, each element consists of more than one process. For example, Fig 2.2 shows a more elaborate *control* system, with all the parts likely to be found in a general system of this type.

Sensors convert physical quantities (measurand) into electronic signals and apply them to the input circuits. In turn, the input circuits convert and amplify the signals if necessary and pass them into the system's control circuits. Here the control circuits process the input information and decide on the appropriate action to be taken. The signals required to produce these actions are sent to the output circuits where the signals are reconverted again and amplified to operate the actuators and/or display devices. Actuators are devices such as solenoid valves, relays and motors that perform an action. Display devices provide visible and/or audible information.

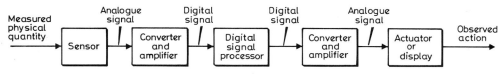

Fig 2.2   Generalized control system

Control loop systems

Any control system can be classified as open-loop or closed-loop. In an open-loop system, the control circuits do not monitor the system's output to determine if the desired control action was achieved (Fig 2.3(a)).

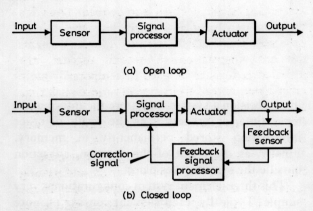

(a) Open loop

(b) Closed loop

Fig 2.3 Block diagrams of
(a) open loop and
(b) closed loop control systems

In a closed-loop system, on the other hand, a feedback sensor and circuit continually monitor the system's output; developing a correction signal, applied to the control circuit, which adjusts the output towards the desired value (Fig 2.3(b)). Generally, control systems comprise only closed-loop designs, as open-loop systems are not accurate due to their very nature.

Microcomputer-based control system

The microprocessor is a very large scale integration (VLSI) circuit whose final function is determined by the sequence of instructions, known as the program, given to it. Individual instructions enable the microprocessor to carry out each step towards completion of a complex circuit function. The basic microprocessor is therefore *not* a dedicated device confined to one particular application, although the majority of microprocessors used for control purposes do have built-in mask-programmable storage circuits which allow them to be dedicated to specific control functions.

The microprocessor can do nothing on its own, requiring a certain amount of supporting hardware, memory and input/out circuits. Fig 2.4 shows the relationship between the four basic functions of microprocessor, memory, input and output. The microprocessor is the central control function for the system, sometimes called the central processing unit (CPU). It performs this processing control function under the direction of instructions stored in the system memory. These instructions make up the system program.

The memory also provides storage of data, function tables, and decision tables. When used for engine management systems it would be programmed with all the information necessary to control functions such as fuel injection quantities and ignition advance characteristics. For example, the memory might contain 16 load and 16 speed

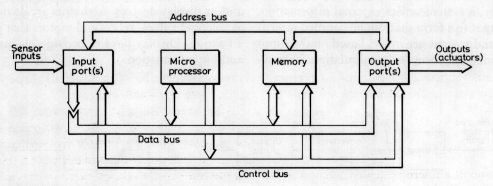

Fig 2.4 A microprocessor-based system

parameters which would permit the use of 256 ignition advance positions based on a combination of these stored values. But the microprocessor has also to consider other parameters when deciding the actual ignition timing point – starting period, coolant temperatures, dwell time, combustion knock, etc.

Input ports allow inputs of system data from sensors and manual controls into the system. The microprocessor interprets the data and implements output control decisions under the guidance of the program stored in memory. Output ports provide the means for the microprocessor to send the output control signal to the device that carries out the desired action.

The microprocessor communicates with the other elements of the internal system by sending digital binary codes along conductors called buses. Initially, the microprocessor may send a binary address code (on the address bus) which determines which input/output port or memory location is to be brought into action. Control signals (on the control bus) are then sent, which determine the direction of data flow (i.e. to or from the microprocessor) and when the transfer of data is to take place. Finally data codes are sent to or from the microprocessor along the data bus.

Each action the microprocessor takes is under the direction of an instruction from memory. Thus, the microprocessor must know where the instruction is located in memory (i.e. its address) and it must fetch the instruction code from memory before the instruction can be carried out. Once inside the microprocessor an instruction decoder circuit interprets the instruction, then a controller generates the required control signals to carry out (execute) the instruction. This sequence of (1) addressing memory and fetching instructions, (2) decoding and executing instructions, is repeated for all instructions in the program.

Basic principles of operation

The operation of a microprocessor is based upon a sequence of instructions which carry out this fetch–execute cycle. Use is made of specific segments of memory, known as registers, which store single words of data or instructions. These registers can be part of the microprocessor itself, or in some instances, part of the general system memory. One register, known as the program counter, is always set to the address of the next location of memory which is to be read. Thus, it's the program counter which lets the microprocessor know which memory address contains the next instruction. A second register, the instruction register, is used to temporarily store an instruction read from memory, until such time as the microprocessor can decode the instruction. Other registers, without specific names, are also used to temporarily store data words.

The fetch operation involves getting an instruction out of a specific memory address, and passing it along the data bus to the microprocessor. In the first part of the fetch cycle the address held in the program counter i.e. the address of the instruction, is transmitted to the memory via the address bus. The memory is set to 'read' by the microprocessor control section, causing the data at the addressed memory location to be put on to the data bus and be transmitted to the microprocessor's instruction register.

After the instruction is decoded the microprocessor increments by 1 the program counter to locate the next portion of the instruction, reads the memory content of that address and stores it in another temporary register. This may continue for a third cycle until the microprocessor has all the information necessary to execute the instruction.

The execute operation involves carrying out the process defined by an instruction. Storage, arithmetic, logical or shift functions are performed on the data during this stage.

After execution of the instruction, the microprocessor fetches the next instruction to be executed, and so on until a halt instruction is executed. The fetch–execute cycle for a typical 8-bit microprocessor takes about 3 microseconds.

Subroutines

A well-structured program contains a number of 'mini' programs or subroutines. Each subroutine is dedicated to a specific task; handling inputs, performing computation, logical data manipulation, or some output function. The instructions within a subroutine are stored and located sequentially in the memory. When the main program requires that a subroutine be performed, an instruction is executed which tells the microprocessor at what address the subroutine is located i.e. the program counter is set to the first instruction location address of the subroutine. The last instruction in the subroutine tells the microprocessor to return to the part of the main program it previously had left.

Memory tables

Automotive electronic control systems have been developed to the stage where complicated charac-

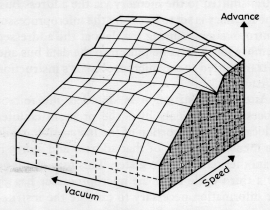

Fig 2.5   Pictorial representation of ignition timing details. Such a representation is stored as tables in system memory

teristic 'diagrams' or 'maps' can be stored in the form of tables in memory. Fig 2.5 shows an example of a possible ignition advance map, illustrating how the ignition advance ideally varies according to vacuum and speed. The map is stored as tables in the system memory. As the microprocessor receives input information regarding vacuum and speed of the engine it can then look up the corresponding ignition advance setting in the table, adjusting the timing to suit.

Memory tables may represent several functions that have to be implemented for control purposes. For example, engine temperature and warm-up times, sensor linearisation, fuel quantity and injection times etc.

Interrupts

Another important function that the microprocessor system can do is respond to high priority signals from the input, output or feedback circuits. These interrupt signals get the immediate attention of the microprocessor, which stops what it was doing and jumps to a subroutine designed to handle the condition that caused the interrupt signal. The importance of the interrupt signalling function is that it allows the microprocessor to handle other jobs without the time consuming job of continually monitoring all circuits. When a circuit needs immediate service it can get the microprocessor's attention by using an interrupt signal. It could be that the ignition is too far advanced and combustion knock is occurring. The knock interrupt signal is fed to the microprocessor, interrupting its normal operation, causing the microprocessor to fetch and execute a subroutine that will retard the ignition timing to prevent further knocking.

3

Sensors

Performance of any control system is, first of all, related to the accuracy with which information about the operating variables or parameters is relayed to the controlling process. The sensors or transducers used to monitor the variables do so by converting (transducing) the variables' physical quantities (measurands) into related electrical signals. Common measurands in automobiles are temperature, pressure, speed, position, flow and oxygen concentration.

Sensors operate in many ways to transduce a measurand into an electrical signal. A knowledge of the methods, their advantages and disadvantages, is essential to the service engineer, who has to check their operating performances.

Temperature sensors

Temperature is an important input variable in engine control systems; in particular with regard to fuel metering and ignition timing, where knowledge of the changing coolant temperature and air temperature is essential. Of the three temperature sensing technologies available; thermocouple, resistive temperature device and thermistor, the thermistor is the one in common usage. A typical temperature sensor consists of a thermistor pellet, mounted in a housing which may be inserted in a fluid or in an air stream.

Thermistors

The thermistor is made of a semiconductor material such as nickel or cobalt oxides, which has a predictable change in resistance as the temperature is changed. On heating the thermistor, electrons break free from the semiconductor's covalent bonds thus reducing the thermistor's resistance (Fig 3.1(a)). The change in resistance with change in temperature is shown in graphical form in Fig 3.1(b). Because the resistance

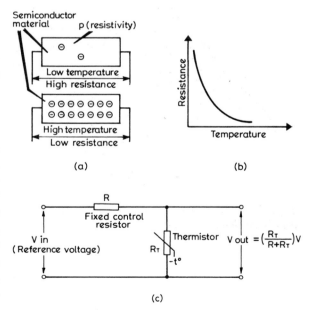

(a)

(b)

(c)

Fig 3.1 (a) *Semiconductor resistance change with temperature*
(b) *Thermistor temperature sensor characteristic*
(c) *Temperature sensor circuit*

decreases with an increase in temperature the thermistor is said to have a negative temperature coefficient (NTC). The resistance change can amount to between 5 and 10% per degrees centigrade, which for a 10 kilohm thermistor element is between about 500 and 10,000 ohm over the operating temperature range of an engine.

Due to this sensitivity, it is possible to make measurements to within 0.05°C, although the relative sensitivity decreases at high temperature changes as shown by the flattening out of the curve in Fig 3.1(b). As the output is only a physical change in resistance it usually has to be changed into a voltage or current. To achieve this the sensor is connected in a circuit to act as part of a potential divider, as shown in Fig 3.1(c), where the voltage drop across the thermistor varies with the change in resistance. Service checks should ensure that the current flow through the thermistor is not high enough to cause self-heating, due to the power dissipated within the thermistor.

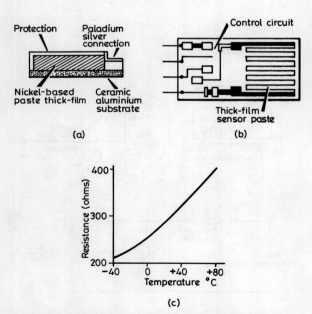

Fig 3.2   Structure and characteristics of a thick-film or temperature sensor
(*a*) *Cross-section*
(*b*) *Plan view*
(*c*) *Resistance-temperature characteristic*

Air temperature

The design principle of the nickel thick-film thermistor (Fig 3.2) makes the device most suitable for sensing intake air temperature. Intake air temperature can change rapidly but the thick-film thermistor's small thermal time constant means that it can still monitor these changes successfully. In addition, it exhibits an almost linear temperature characteristic curve (Fig 3.2(c)).

In some electronic control systems a negative temperature coefficient thermocouple is used to measure the inside wall temperature of the inlet manifold. The inside wall temperature of the inlet manifold is really a mixed value comprising manifold wall and fuel-air mixture temperatures – the value being used to influence the volume of fuel to be supplied by an electronic carburettor.

Thermocouples

The thermocouple works on the principle that a voltage is generated by a circuit comprising two junctions of two dissimilar metals (Fig 3.3). When one of the junctions is kept at a constant temperature the voltage change of the circuit is a function of the temperature change at the other junction, and is linearly related. With an operating range of 250°C to 2000°C they are most useful for measuring exhaust gas and turbocharger temperatures.

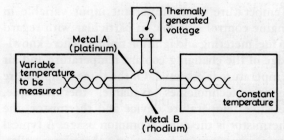

Fig 3.3   Thermocouple temperature sensing principle

Intake air mass sensors

To accurately control the air-fuel ratio it is necessary to measure the intake air mass exactly. The mass of air per kilogram of fuel in a mixture of air and fuel gives the air-fuel ratio of the mixture. For the complete combustion of an air-petrol mixture the ratio is approximately 15 parts of air to 1 part of fuel (15:1) by mass. By measuring the mass of air drawn into a cylinder, the correct mass of fuel for complete burning can be determined and injected.

Currently, two methods are used to measure intake air mass. One of these measures the air mass indirectly by measuring the inlet manifold pressure; the other measures the air mass directly. Both methods must compensate for changes in air density caused by ambient temperature and altitude variations.

Absolute pressure sensors

When the engine is running, the inlet manifold pressure varies from nearly zero with the throttle valve closed to almost atmospheric pressure when the throttle valve is fully open. Therefore manifold absolute pressure can be used as an indication of the load operating conditions of the engine, and hence the air-fuel ratio to satisfy the operating condition.

Aneroid absolution sensor

The basic aneroid is a sealed, evacuated chamber, rigid except for one end which is a thin plate that can flex easily. The thin plate, acting as a diaphragm, deflects according to the pressure exerted on it, in this case manifold pressure. Fig 3.4(a) shows a cross-section of a typical pressure sensor formed by two evacuated aneroids and suitable mechanisms for converting diaphragm deflection into electrical signals. In practice two methods are used for this conversion:

(1) Linear variable differential transformer (LVDT) – as shown in Fig 3.4(a)

The LVDT has a moveable core attached to the diaphragm. When the diaphragm is deflected by manifold pressure change it varies the output of the transformer. The primary section of the transformer comprises an oscillator and primary wind-

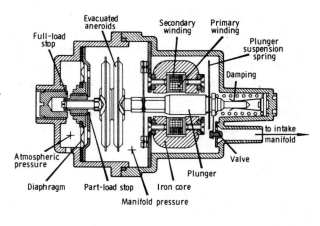

(a)

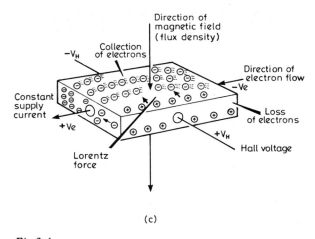

(b)

(c)

Fig 3.4
(a) *Aneroid chamber-type absolute pressure sensor using an LVDT transducer*
(b) *LVDT principle*
(c) *Hall effect principle*

ing to create an alternating magnetic flux (Fig 3.4(b)). The output (secondary) windings are centre tapped to give two balanced coils with equal output when the transformer core is in the central position. The secondary coils are not only equal but are of opposing polarities, so they cancel each other out, and the output voltage is zero. As the core is displaced from the central position by manifold pressure, the output voltage of one winding is more than the other, so that the output voltage varies in direct proportion to the position of the core. A separate signal processing circuit produces an analogue DC voltage proportional to the manifold pressure.

(2) Hall effect detector

When electrons move through a semiconductor layer (Fig 3.4(c)), perpendicular to the lines of flux of a magnetic field, an electromagnetic force (the Lorentz force) acts on each electron perpendicular to the direction of current flow. As the result of this force, electrons drift to one side of the semiconductor causing a surplus of electrons and a negative polarity at this side, and a depletion of electrons and a positive polarity at the other side. The voltage generated across the two sides due to this Hall effect is known as the Hall voltage, and the stronger the magnetic field the higher the Hall voltage.

In pressure sensors using a Hall effect detector, the deflection of the diaphragm moves the position of a permanent magnet causing a change of magnetic field strength acting on a Hall semiconductor element (Fig 3.4(c)). The Hall voltage generated by the semiconductor element is directly proportional to the magnetic field strength and thus the inlet manifold pressure.

Capacitive absolute pressure sensor

This is another sensor that uses an evacuated chamber, but has two thin metal diaphragms which act as the plates of a capacitor, as shown in Fig 3.5(a). The plates are insulated from the chamber by a dielectric material and the capacitor capsule is inside a sealed housing which is connected to manifold pressure.

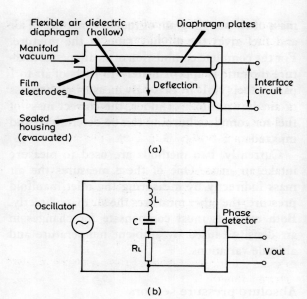

Fig 3.5   Capacitive absolute pressure sensor
(a) Construction
(b) Detecting circuit

As the plates deflect with manifold pressure variation, the capacitance of the capsule changes because the distance between the plates varies. Capacitance increases (distance decreases) as manifold pressure increases. The capacitance is measured by connecting the capsule into a series resonant circuit and applying an AC signal of known frequency and amplitude from an oscillator, as shown in Fig 3.5(b). The oscillator frequency is the same as the circuit's resonant frequency of atmospheric (absolute manifold) pressure. At this balanced frequency the voltage across the inductor and capacitor sensor are equal, but of opposite phase and so cancel each other out. At a manifold pressure equal to atmospheric pressure, therefore, the full supply voltage is applied across the resistor and a zero output is given from the phase detector. As the manifold pressure decreases, the capacitance falls, the circuit's resonant frequency changes and a voltage is created across the resistor. The phase of the resistor voltage varies sharply relative to the reference phase. The phase detector detects the change in phase and supplies an output voltage proportional to the change in phase and hence proportional to manifold pressure.

Semiconductor absolute pressure sensor

The semiconductor absolute pressure sensor comprises a diaphragm of n-type silicon, with four piezoresistors diffused in it, connected to form a Wheatstone bridge (Fig 3.6). The resistors are

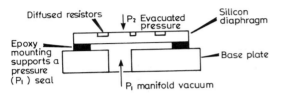

Fig 3.6 *Basic construction of a semiconductor absolute pressure sensor*

formed by diffusing an impurity element into the n-silicon diaphragm, thereby forming a diffused strain gauge. The piezoresistors are formed around the edge of the diaphragm, two radially and two tangentially. The set-up is sealed and an evacuated chamber is formed between the glass plate and the central area of the silicon diaphragm. External connections to the resistors are made with fine gold wires connected to the metal bonding pads. This complete assembly is placed in a sealed housing which is connected to the manifold by a small bore tube.

A piezoresistor is made from a material in which the resistance changes, with a change in twisting or bending force, due to stress in the material, thus providing a variable resistance output. Fig 3.7 shows the circuit diagram used with this type of sensor. The semiconductor bridge is supplied with a constant voltage, and a current of approximately 1 mA. When there is no strain on the diaphragm all four resistances are equal, the bridge is balanced and the output voltage from the bridge is zero. As the stress of applied pressure causes the diaphragm to deflect, the resulting strain on the piezoresistors causes them to change in value; in such a way that R_1 and R_4 (tangential resistors) increase in value proportional to pressure because they are being compressed and at the

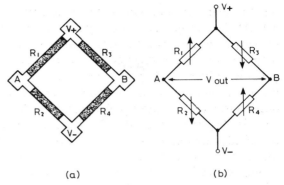

(a)   (b)

Fig 3.7 *Piezoresistor Wheatstone bridge arrangement for the semiconductor absolute pressure sensor*
(a) *Piezoresistor bridge diffused in silicon diaphragm*
(b) *Piezoresistors in Wheatstone bridge form*

same time R_2 and R_3 decrease in value by the same amount as these resistors (radial resistors) are being elongated. This unbalances the bridge and a voltage difference is created at the bridge terminals, which in turn lowers the mid-point voltage of the R_1 R_2 divider (point A) and raises the midpoint voltage of the R_3 and R_4 divider (point B), resulting in a change in voltage between A and B which is proportional to the pressure change. Since this output is about 50 mV/80 kPa, and rather small for control systems, it is amplified to several volts at 80 kPa by an operational amplifier.

Potentiometer air flow sensor

A sensor plate, mounted on a pivot shaft in the sensor housing and loaded by a calibrated coil spring, protrudes into the air inlet recess (Fig 3.8). The higher the rate of air flow the more the sensor plate is rotated. To steady the sensor plate, a compensation plate swings simultaneously in a damping housing to provide a smooth action. The rotating sensor plate is connected to a potentiometer (not shown), the output of which is a voltage signal corresponding to the angle of deflection. The potentiometer in such a sensor is made using thick-film techniques, with a ceramic substrate onto which a potentiometer track of wear-resistant material is overlaid. To obtain the required output characteristic, the potentiometer is 'fine tuned' by baking onto the substrate several

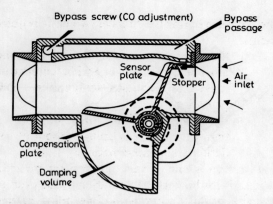

Fig 3.8   *Potentiometer air flow sensor principle*

film resistors of ceramic metal (cermet) which are connected to sections of the track by very narrow conductive straps.

When measuring the quantity of air drawn into the cylinder of an engine using an air flow sensor of this type an error is introduced, depending on the altitude, which must be compensated for. This sensor is also prone to pulsation errors and the moving parts are subject to wear.

Measuring intake air mass flow indirectly by the means we have seen here is quite inaccurate, because the air volume is determined by the air pressure and temperature at a point in the manifold, so the measured air mass differs from the air mass actually charged into the cylinder. This can be minimised by using a more direct measuring method.

Direct air flow sensors

Compared with indirect pressure sensing methods direct measurement of air mass flow detects air flow quickly and accurately. This allows highly accurate control of the air-fuel ratio, which is a most important factor in improving combustion.

Hot-wire air flow sensor

Hot-wire anemometry is a well established method for measuring mass flow. It involves placing a very thin resistance wire, of 50–100 μm diameter, in the air stream, heating it to a very high temperature by means of an electric current

and detecting changes in the electric current (500–1200 mA) due to heat transfer from the hot-wire to the cold-air stream. A typical sensor construction is shown in Fig 3.9(a).

The small wire-wound sensing probe is placed in a by-pass channel of the inlet air path, which has its outlet at the venturi port. The pressure

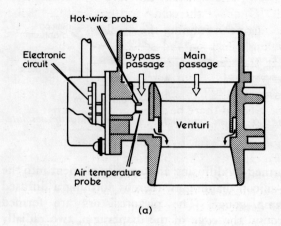

(a)

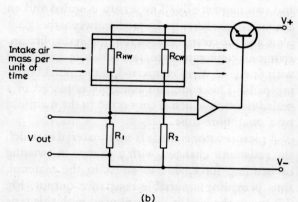

(b)

Fig 3.9   *Hot-wire air mass flow sensor*
(a) *Typical configuration*
(b) *Control circuit*

difference between the inlet and outlet of the by-pass channel achieves an air flow which is proportional to that of the main inlet air flow path. Another sensing probe with the same construction as the hot-wire probe is also installed in the by-pass measuring channel, and is used to measure the inlet air temperature to compensate for temperature variations. The compensating wire is called a 'cold-wire' and has negligible current passing through it. The air-flow sensor also determines the temperature and density of the air by measuring the resistance of the hot-wire probe.

Initially, the sensing wire has a controlled current flowing through it to raise its temperature to a known and constant difference in temperature (100 °C) above the cold-wire temperature. When the engine is running the air flow velocity has a cooling effect on the sensing wire, due to the heat transfer from resistor to air, reducing its resistance. The current is increased to keep the resistance and temperature at the constant difference. Should there be a change in resistance of the cold-wire due to air temperature, this will be compensated for by further regulating the hot-wire current. The changing current required to maintain the constant temperature difference is proportional to the air flow velocity, temperature and density of the incoming air.

The two wire probes usually form part of a conventional bridge configuration as shown in Fig 3.9(b). In this circuit the hot-wire sensing probe is used as one of the resistors (R_{HW}) on one branch of the bridge, while the cold-wire resistor (R_{CW}) is used on the other branch: when balanced the bridge voltage is zero. The unbalanced voltage of the bridge is amplified and fed, via a transistor, back into the bridge circuit, so that when the temperature of the hot-wire falls and its resistance decreases, the circuit acts so as to increase the voltage applied to the bridge and so increase the current in the hot-wire resistor, thereby raising its temperature to the correct level. The control circuit is constantly balanced and maintains the relationship:

$$R_2 R_{HW} = R_1 R_{CW}$$

It is important that the controlled current flow is not affected by air temperature, but depends solely on the air flow velocity. Therefore the resistance of the hot-wire probe is proportional to the difference between the hot-wire velocity temperature and the cold-wire temperature, giving full temperature compensation. The resistor for the hot-wire sensor has to meet two basic requirements:

1   the temperature coefficient of resistance must be constant over a wide temperature range, to facilitate temperature compensation
2   the surface condition must be stable so that little change is brought about by oxidation and contamination.

Platinum is one of very few resistor materials that satisfies both these conditions. But even so, contamination of the wire surface still sometimes occurs and some control circuits counteract this by heating the wire to a much higher temperature (1000 °C) for, say, 1 second every time the engine is switched off. This action burns off any dirt and contaminants on the hot wire.

When the mass of air drawn by the engine is measured directly by the hot wire method the measurements are independent of changes in the density of the air.

Vortex airflow sensor

This sensor uses the phenomenon of Karmen Vortex Street and comprises an air channel with a triangular strut, ultrasonic transmitter and receiver to detect the vortexes and an electronic control and signal processing circuit. The basic structure of the sensor is shown in Fig 3.10.

When the inlet air passes through the air channel vortexes are generated in the wake of the triangular strut, the frequency of which is nearly proportional to the airflow velocity in the air channel, therefore air velocity (volumetric airflow quantity) can be measured by measuring the vortex frequency.

In this type of sensor bymorph-type ceramic ultrasonic transducers, composed of titanate-zirconia-lead (PZT), are used for both the ultrasonic transmitter and receiver. The control circuit uses a feedback oscillator operating at about 40 kHz to energise the ultrasonic transmitter. The ultrasonic wave from the transmitter passes through the airflow containing the vortexes before it reaches the receiver. Thus the frequency and amplitude of the ultrasonic waves are periodically varied (modu-

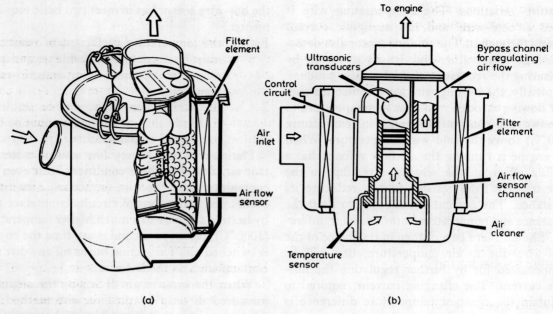

Fig 3.10 Vortex air flow sensor
(a) Cutaway

(b) Cross-section

lated) by the strength of the vortexes. The received wave is demodulated and converted into an alternating signal or rectangular waves (pulses), the amplitude of which corresponds to the circulating strength of the vortexes and the frequency of which corresponds to the number of vortexes generated. The output frequency is around 30 to 50 Hz at idling condition, and reaches 1.0 to 1.5 kHz at full load.

This airflow sensor as described above, measures volumetric airflow rate, so that output data have to be converted to the mass airflow rate for application to a fuel metering system. An inlet air temperature sensor is incorporated for this purpose. Also a barometric pressure sensor would be used for the correction if operated at high altitudes.

Air and oil pressure sensors

Many of the sensing methods described earlier can be used for air and oil pressure sensing.

Air pressure sensing

Measurement of this parameter permits detection of either a moderate air leak or a sudden failure in the air supply of an air braking system, as well as monitoring the working pressure.

Aneroid LVDT pressure sensor
The metal diaphragms provide an almost linear displacement with gauge pressure. The aneroid capsule vents to atmospheric pressure and drives a linear variable transformer, or other device, which outputs a voltage proportion to gauge pressure.

Potentiometric sensor
This is widely used since it is simply a diaphragm driving a potentiometer. Although it is of low cost and has a high level output, it has moving parts that wear out, change its calibration and cause failure. The above two sensors are now being replaced by more reliable sensors that have fewer moving parts and no frictional contact.

Capacitive pressure sensor

In the common approach, the capacitive pressure sensor is circular and composed of an aluminium diaphragm bonded to a thicker aluminium substrate to form the capacitive plates. A conductive electrode is screened on each plate. When pressure is applied to the diaphragm it deflects towards the substrate, causing decrease in capacitance.

Semiconductor pressure sensors

This sensor uses a silicon diaphragm and diffused piezoresistors, instead of a discrete potentiometer. When pressure is applied to the diaphragm the resistance changes in proportion to the twisting or bending force on the material. See absolute pressure sensors for full details.

Thick-film pressure sensors

Similar in design and construction to the semiconductor diaphragm type, but instead of using a silicon diaphragm and diffused piezoresistor, its diaphragm is aluminium and the resistors are thick-film piezoresistor (mainly glass and metal oxides). The thick-film material's resistance decreases in compression and increases in tension as the diaphragm deflects under applied pressure. The relative change in resistance is linear in the whole range of the applied strain.

Oil pressure sensing

Oil pressure is one of the most important variables to be measured on an engine, ideally requiring the use of a continuous oil pressure sensor rather than a pressure switch. The sensing methods used in oil pressure sensors are similar to those used in air pressure sensing, although oil pressure sensors require a higher temperature range (130°C) because the sensor is mounted directly on the engine block. Also the pressure required to give full scale deflections are different, typically lower in the oil pressure sensor. The various pressure ranges are obtained by changing the geometrical dimension of the diaphragm. The output from either the oil or air sensor can be a voltage or resistance change.

Fuel flow rate sensors

Accurate measurement of fuel flow rate is essential to a real time computation of economy, and parameters of driver information systems. However a measurement of fuel flow rate is not really possible in the diesel engine, where the fuel flow rate does not correspond to the actual amount of fuel used – a substantial amount of the fuel supplied to the injectors is for cooling purposes and a return fuel flow system is employed. Therefore the methods described here are only suitable for petrol engine vehicles.

Turbine flowmeter

The turbine flowmeter has a long history of use for accurate measurement of liquid flow and, only recently, has been adapted for automotive use. This type of sensor uses a turbine whose impeller (rotor) is activated by fuel flowing tangentially (Fig 3.11(a)) or axially (Fig 3.11(b)) through it.

The sensor is fitted into the fuel feed line to the carburettor and produces a fixed number of pulses for every litre of fuel passing through. Generally, flowmeters work on the light interruptor principle, such that as the fuel flows through the turbine

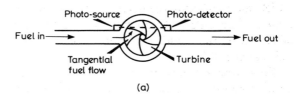

(a)

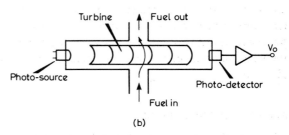

(b)

Fig 3.11   Turbine flowmeter
(a) *Tangential*
(b) *Axial*

unit it causes the turbine impeller to rotate and interrupt a beam of light transmitted by a LED and received by a phototransistor. The number of pulses produced is proportional to the amount of fuel flowing past the turbine. The voltage pulse output is a square wave switching between earth (0V) and vehicle voltage (12V).

The axial turbine attempts to solve the problem of bubbles being recognised as fuel by using the fact that light may be refracted through the fuel. When the turbine is full of fuel the sensor is aligned so that the light beam is refracted through the fuel from LED to phototransistor. When a bubble occupies the space between consecutive impeller blades the light is not refracted enough to reach the phototransistor, so to the sensor it appears that the turbine has not turned. Large bubbles are therefore not counted even though the rotor turns when they and fuel pass through.

Ball-in-race flowmeter

The ball-in-race flowmeter uses an opaque ball which is propelled around a toroidal channel by the fuel being measured. Each time the ball passes around the toroid it interrupts a light beam, generating a pulsed output signal as in Fig 3.12.

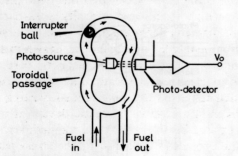

Fig 3.12   Ball-in-race flowrate sensor

Displacement flowmeter

The general operating principle of this type of flowmeter is the charging and discharging of a fixed volume of liquid in a chamber. The measured frequency of the cycle of operation is multiplied by the volume to give the flow rate. The

simplest concepts for this sensor are a rotary type hydraulic motor gearpump or a piston moving in a chamber.

Piston flowmeter

Consists of four radial pistons connected to the same crankshaft, each piston acting as a valve mechanism, directing fuel flow to and from the adjacent pistons, with the magnitude and direction of rotation of the crankshaft being sensed by a photoelectric transmitter or magnetic tachometer, Fig 3.13.

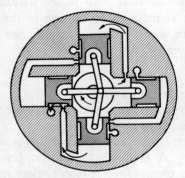

Fig 3.13   Four piston positive flow rate sensor

Gear flowmeter

In this concept a gear pump converts the flow measurement into a differential pressure measurement. The gear pump is in line with the fuel flow and is driven by the fuel at such a speed that the average differential pressure across the pump is zero. Under this condition the pump becomes a positive displacement hydraulic rotor. To obtain the output signal the rotational speed of the shafts is sensed by a magnetic pick up and is a measure of the fuel flow rate.

Motion sensors

Many automotive functions to be controlled are concerned with motions:

1   Crankshaft rotation, where it is necessary to know both rotational speed and angular position

2 Road wheel speed, where both absolute and differential values are needed if wheel lock is to be detected

3 Transmission shaft speed, where the information is used to select transmission ratios or maintain a constant cruising speed or provide trip information for the driver.

A number of attractive technologies have been used which meet the stringent automotive requirements. All have some advantage and disadvantage which affect their quality of performance and serviceability.

Hall effect sensors

When used to sense speed or position a Hall semiconductor element may be placed between the poles of a permanent magnet system. When a current flows through the semiconductor element a Hall voltage is generated at right angles to the current flow and perpendicular to the direction of the magnetic flux. The value of the Hall voltage is proportional to the product of the magnetic field strength and the current. If one of these quantities is held constant then the Hall voltage generated will be directly proportional to the other variable quantity. In motion sensing it is the strength of the magnetic field that is varied, and the control current is held constant, hence the Hall voltage is proportional to the magnetic field strength.

The Hall sensor is wear free and produces a constant output voltage throughout the system's life. Also, the output voltage remains predictable over a wide frequency range although the *accuracy* of the voltage is dependent upon the constancy of the magnetic field and the exciting current. The Hall sensor can detect zero motion and is ideal for application to odometer systems, driver information systems, and ignition timing position systems. The generated Hall voltage is relatively weak so it is normally amplified and processed by electronic devices built into the Hall semiconductor chip.

Optical sensors

Component speed and position can also be sensed using optical methods. If an aperture disc is positioned between a light source and a photo-electric detector then a signal will be generated as the disc is rotated and the detector is alternatively illuminated and blocked. The light need not be visible and can range from infra-red to ultra violet. Generally, a LED and phototransistor are used as light source and detector. The resultant signals are timed reference and may be used to sense position, flow and speed of rotation. There are two limitations, however, that must be taken into account when testing such sensors for faults or when checking their calibration co-efficients. First, as both light source and detector are semiconductors there is a temperature limitation. Second, there may also be the problem of obscuration due to accumulated dirt.

Wiegand sensors

This is an interesting type of sensor which is now finding wide application in vehicle electronic systems. Named after the person who discovered and announced it (John R. Wiegand), the Wiegand Effect is the name given to a magnetic phenomenon which occurs in a specially work-hardened small diameter ferro-magnetic wire. The wire is approximately 0.3 mm diameter, drawn in such a manner as to give it a soft magnetic core and a hard magnetic outer sheath. The whole structure is then subjected to a longitudinal twisting force, to make it a bistable magnetic device; that is, it can exist stably in either of two magnetic states due to the properties locked in by the stress patterns created during the twisting process. The direction of magnetisation changes quite abruptly when the wire is exposed to a sufficiently strong external magnetic field.

In its original state both core and sheath are polarised in the same direction and this is maintained in a field free condition due to the permantly magnetised sheath (Fig 3.14(a)). When the wire core is exposed to an opposing magnetic field the soft magnetic centre magnetically switches (Fig 3.14(b)), but returns to its original direction when the magnetic field is removed. In a typical Wiegand sensor arrangement (Fig 3.14(c)) a sensing coil is wound around the Wiegand wire and allows the switching field to be detected. The multi-fingered vane rotates in a horizontal plane to interrupt the magnetic field and cause the Wiegand wire to switch. The lower permanent magnet provides the positive saturating flux to the Wiegand wire. The upper magnet, whose field the

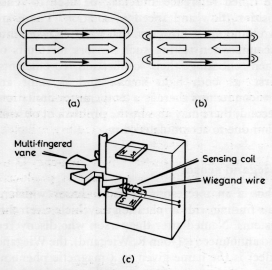

(a)   *(b)*

(c)

Fig 3.14   Wiegand effect and sensor
(a)   Wiegand wire in unswitched state
(b)   Switched Wiegand wire
(c)   Typical Wiegand sensor arrangement

fingers of the vane interrupt, provides the negative saturating flux. This symmetrical magnet field arrangement generates an output signal with equal positive and negative pulses. The positive pulse occurs when the leading edge of a vane finger enters the slot of the Wiegand module and the negative pulse occurs when the trailing edge leaves the module. A typical sensing coil has around 1300 turns and the induced potential, on open circuit, is between 2.0 and 2.5V, with a pulse width of twenty microseconds at half amplitude. The value of the induced voltage is almost independent of the rate of change of flux reversal.

When testing it must be remembered that a change of flux polarity is required. A change of field strength of the same polarity will not produce a signal.

The Wiegand Sensor is an effective transducer for providing digital pulses in response to motion or displacement, typical automotive applications include: ignition triggers; speed signals for speedometer and tachometer drive; crankshaft speed and position; flowmeter; wheel sensor for anti-skid systems; and transmission control signals.

Inductive sensors

An inductive sensor consists of a sensing coil and a permanent magnet, forming a closed magnetic circuit (Fig 3.15(a)). The permanent magnet creates a magnetic flux in the magnetic circuit, the value of which depends on the field strength of the magnet and on the reluctance of the magnetic circuit. When the air gap of the magnet is bridged by the finger of a vaned rotor or similar impulse, the reluctance is reduced and the magnetic flux increases (Fig 3.15(b)).

This induces a voltage across the sensing coil, the polarity of which depends on the direction of the change of magnetic field, controlled by the

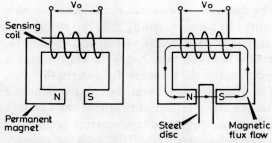

(a) Air gap, high reluctance to magnetic flux flow, no induction in sensing coil

(b) Metal disc between poles of magnet, low reluctance and magnetic flux flows round the circuit inducing a voltage into the sensing coil

Fig 3.15   Basic structure and principle of an inductive sensor
(a)   High reluctance to magnetic flux, no induction in sensing coil
(b)   Impulse finger cuts air gap, low reluctance and hence an induced voltage in sensing coil

polarity of the permanent magnet, the winding direction of the coil, and whether the reluctance is increasing or decreasing. Note the rotational direction of the impulse wheel does *not* influence the polarity of the output voltage.

Since the value of output voltage is proportional to the number of winding turns and the rate of change of the magnetic flux. This means that the output voltage of the inductive sensor is proportional to the rate of transition of reluctance and, hence, the speed with which the impulse finger cuts, or even passes close by, the air gap of the magnet.

Permanently magnetised inductive sensors such as described here are common, but other versions of inductive sensors are also used.

AC excited inductive sensor

If a toothed impulse wheel is rotated close to an inductive sensor, whose coil is excited by an alternating current, there will be a periodic change in the coil's impedance and the AC signal through the coil will be modulated. This modulation may be used to determine rotational angle and speed. Fig 3.16 shows a typical AC excited inductive sensor arrangement. This type of sensor has the advantage of being able to detect zero motion.

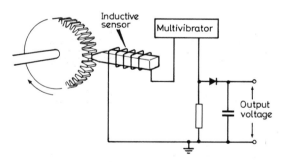

Fig 3.16   AC excited inductive sensor

DC excited inductive sensors

Magnetic field strength in this sensor is controlled by passing direct current through the coil, allowing control of the output voltage to a set maximum value, irrespective of impulse speed (Fig 3.17).

These sensors are used where high rotational

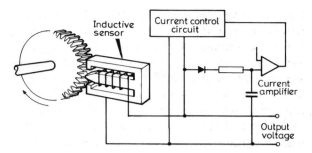

Fig 3.17   DC excited inductive sensor

speeds or fast changes of rotational angles have to be measured. Currently they are used for diagnostic and service adjustments of ignition angles and injection timing.

Quenched oscillator speed sensor

This sensor is basically a pulse generator, consisting of an inductive sensor, control circuit and a four pole rotor which is connected to a vehicle's drive shaft (Fig 3.18(a)).

The oscillator produces a high frequency (3 to 4 MHz) signal whenever a voltage is produced across the sensing coil of the inductive sensor. Thus, as the rotor blades pass the sensor the

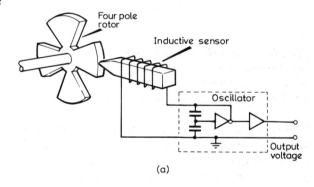

(a)

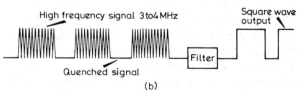

(b)

Fig 3.18   Quenched oscillator speed sensor
(a) Typical arrangement
(b) Resultant output signal, before and after filtering

oscillator is turned on and off i.e. the high frequency signal is quenched as each rotor blade passes the sensor (Fig 3.18(b)). A filter filters out the high frequency signal to produce a regular square wave pulse.

Feedback sensors

Closed-loop control using feedback makes it possible to maintain engine variables very precisely: in particular the point of ignition and air-fuel ratio – both of which have a critical effect on fuel economy and exhaust gas emission levels. Two main types of feedback sensors are used: lambda oxygen sensors – to create feedback signals regarding instantaneous mixture composition; knock sensors – providing feedback signals when detonation occurs.

Lambda oxygen sensor

With this type of sensor signal generation is based on measuring the residual oxygen in the exhaust gas. The name originates from the Greek letter (λ) which is used to denote the equivalence ratio or excess air factor.

Power, fuel and exhaust gas composition of the SI engine are all dependent on the composition of the air-fuel mixture. Complete combustion occurs with an air-fuel ratio of approximately 15:1, or its equivalent ratio ($\lambda = 1$), where:

$$\lambda = \frac{\text{actual quantity of air}}{\text{theoretical air requirement}}$$

or

$$\lambda = \frac{\text{actual air-fuel ratio}}{\text{theoretically correct air-fuel ratio (14.7:1)}}$$

so that when the actual air quantity or air-fuel ratio supplied to the cylinder equals the theoretical requirement λ will equal 1 (100% combustion efficiency). It then follows when insufficient air (a rich mixture) is supplied λ will be less than 1, and with excess air (a lean mixture) λ will be greater than 1.

Fig 3.19(a) shows graphically the relationship between levels of various compounds within the

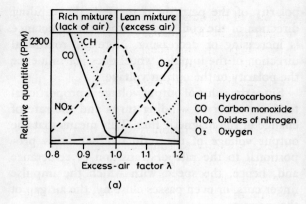

(a)

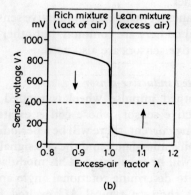

(b)

Fig 3.19   Excess air factor and
(a) Effect on exhaust gas composition
(b) Typical lambda oxygen sensor output voltages

cylinder gases and λ. If an engine is supplied with the correct mixture of petrol and air ($CH + O_2N_2$), the exhaust gases should consist of a mixture of carbon dioxide, water vapour and nitrogen ($CO_2 + H_2O + N_2$). Due to various factors combustion may not be 100% efficient and oxygen will be present in the exhaust gases.

Sensors which measure the amount of oxygen present in exhaust gases, and hence determine the air-fuel mixture, are known as exhaust gas oxygen (EGO) sensors and generate a voltage (Fig 3.19(b)), dependent on the air-fuel ratio which can be used to feed back information to enable virtually complete combustion to take place. Two types of material are used for EGO sensors; zirconia oxide (ZrO_2) and titanium oxide (TiO_2).

The operation of EGO sensors depends on the

porosity of the material which allows diffusion of oxygen ions in the exhaust gas. When a difference occurs between two sensing plates a voltage is generated. This voltage changes sharply at $\lambda = 1$ and is the basis of the sensor's feedback signal.

Zirconia oxide

The principal operation is based on the ceramic material's ability to conduct oxygen ions which accumulate on the ZrO_2 surface. Two sensing probes are used, one is reference to the oxygen content of ambient air at normal atmospheric pressure; the other is exposed to the exhaust gas and senses that part of the gas pressure caused by the oxygen content. The exhaust gas oxygen partial pressure for a rich mixture varies over the range 10^{-16} to 10^{-32} of atmospheric pressure. For a lean mixture this is around 10^{-2} atmospheric pressure. If the oxygen proportions at the two sensing probes are equal the output voltage will be zero. But, when the oxygen content at each ZrO_2 probe differs, a voltage is generated across the two. The electrolytic action which generates this voltage is shown in Fig 3.20(a), where the negative oxygen ions under atmospheric pressure permeate the porous electrode and accumulate on its surface, giving it a negative charge the size of which is dependent upon the amount of oxygen in the exhaust gas.

Titanium oxide

Titanium oxide exhaust gas sensors need no reference to ambient air. Titanium oxide is a semiconductor with a very high resistivity at room temperature when it is pure and in air. Loss of oxygen results in molecular vacancies which act as electron donors. As the oxygen content decreases, more electrons become 'free' for electrical conduction, and the material's resistivity decreases. At low oxygen concentrations the TiO_2 material is an n-type semiconductor. At ambient air oxygen concentrations the material has maximum resistance. Beyond this point the material becomes a p-type semiconductor. Thus, the resistance of the TiO_2 oxygen sensor changes very rapidly when the air-fuel ratio changes from rich to weak and vice versa.

The TiO_2 sensor (Fig 3.20(b)) requires some form of temperature compensation. In practice two series elements are used

1 the oxygen-sensing porous TiO_2 ceramic semiconductor
2 a densified TiO_2 ceramic used as a matched thermistor for temperature compensation.

EGO sensor construction

Both types of sensors can be positioned into exhaust manifold or tailpipe, and are generally heated to normal operating temperature by the

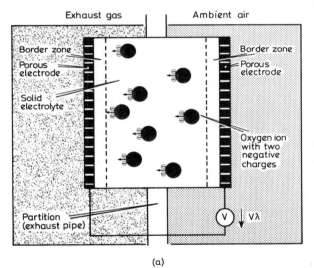

(a)

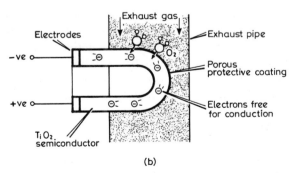

(b)

Fig 3.20   Principles of lambda oxygen sensor used as exhaust gas oxygen (EGO sensors)
(a)   Zirconia oxide EGO sensor
(b)   Titanium oxide EGO sensor

exhaust gas. The voltage and internal resistance of the sensors are temperature dependent and reliable operation typically occurs at temperatures over 300°C. The construction of both types of sensors are shown in Fig. 3.21.

Sensor temperature is a decisive factor with respect to the quality of emission control. The sensor must be positioned in the exhaust system

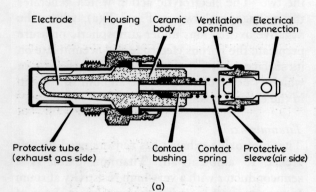

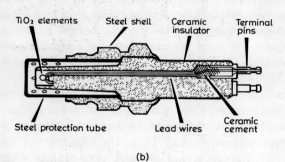

Fig 3.21   Construction of exhaust gas oxygen sensors
(a) Zirconia oxide
(b) Titanium oxide

so as to ensure that the sensor's active element reaches 280–300°C within 30 seconds of engine start-up. To achieve this the sensor is usually very close to the engine exhaust manifold but the position must also ensure that element does not exceed 850°C or severe aging of the electrode will occur. In many engines it is difficult to find the optimum installation position to give a temperature range between 500 and 800°C over the entire operating range from idle to full load. The introduction of a heating element which projects

into the inside of the Zirconia element, make it possible for the EGO sensor to be installed in *any* position of the exhaust system. The heating element is designed to operate at a nominal 13 volts and provide rapid heat-up of the sensor from cold. Power consumption is about 9 watts at 850°C.

Knock sensors

The charge of air-fuel mixture in the engine cylinder should burn quickly to permit optimum performance and high speed but, equally so, it should burn progressively, smoothly and not *too* quickly to create early detonation i.e. knocking of the engine. There are many factors which may lead to knocking combustion; different fuel qualities; advanced ignition timing; aging and environmental effect. A knocking combustion process leads to an extremely sharp rise in cylinder pressure and produces pressure oscillation. Depending on its intensity the piston and crank components may be overloaded, or the engine may overheat and lead to serious mechanical damage. The use of knock sensors enables an engine to run on the threshold of 'knock' and should knock occur the sensor feeds the information back to an electronic control unit which retards the ignition timing to reduce the knock detected.

Various technologies have been used to sense the vibrations associated with knocking pressure frequencies and convert them into electrical voltage signals. For automotive use accelerometer sensors appear to be the most suitable: where piezo-ceramic materials are used as the active elements to measure the structure-borne vibration of the engine. Their high natural frequencies and almost linear sensing of the vibration frequencies up to more than 15 kHz provide ideal information that can be analysed for knocking.

The piezo-ceramic active element usually consists of lead, zirconia and titanium which gives a piezo-electrical activity up to 360°C. Typical sensor construction is shown in Fig 3.22. This style of construction enables the sensor to be easily attached to the most favourable point (a knock

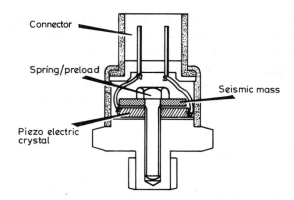

Fig 3.22   Construction of piezo-electric accelerometer, knock sensor

resonant site) on the engine for measuring knock. Where one sensor is used it is positioned between the centre two cylinders. More than one sensor would be placed between two cylinder groupings.

Piezo-electric devices produce a voltage when the ceramic crystals are subjected to mechanical stress variations. This coupling between mechanical and electrical energy generates voltage across opposite faces, proportional to the cause of the stress variations. The seismic mass of the sensor is initially torqued down to pre-stress the piezo-electric sensing element. This allows the piezo-electric crystal to also act as a spring. As a knock occurs in the engine cylinder, it is transmitted via the engine block to the sensor, causing the seismic mass-piezo-electric crystal spring arrangement to vibrate in sympathy. Resultant deformation of the piezo-electric crystals generates an output voltage proportional to the original knock.

Output voltage is typically 10–25 mV/g giving a voltage sensitivity of 25 mV for every 9.81 m/s of acceleration (g). The sensor is mounted by the integral stud and to maintain sensitivity maximum torque values must not be exceeded.

Pressure vibration frequencies other than the typical knock frequency are also contained in the structure-borne vibration signal. The characteristic knocking signal must be electronically extracted from other signals, then analysed by an evaluation circuit, the result of which is supplied

to the electronic control unit, which decides whether or not to retard the ignition point of next combustion in a particular cylinder.

Fluid level sensors

Fluid level sensors are used to sense information about all fluid containers on the vehicle.

Resistive types

A common application is the float-type level transmitter using a thick film resistive track and wiper. Fig 3.23(a) shows a typical sensor. Fig 3.23(b) shows circuits for low fuel warning, incorporated within the sensor itself. When there is sufficient

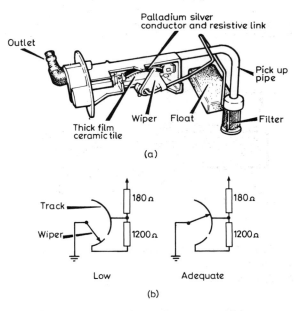

Fig 3.23   Fuel volume sensor
(a) Construction
(b) Arrangement of track resistances to activate low fuel warning

fuel the resistance between ground and the terminal to the control circuit is 180 ohms. This value changes to 1380 ohms, however, when the fuel level is low – the control circuit detects this large change and issues a low fuel warning to the driver, when about 5 to 8 litres of fuel are left.

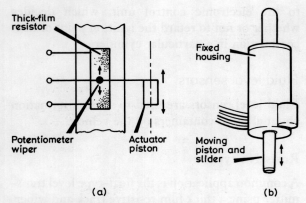

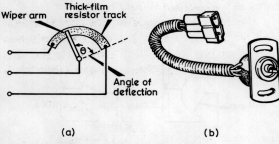

Fig 3.24   Linear deflection sensor
(a) Principle   (b) Construction

Fig 3.24 shows the principle and typical construction of a resistive sensor for measuring the linear deflection of a vehicle, which may be used as input data for a headlamp levelling system – useful if the vehicle is loaded. Fig 3.25 shows the principle and construction of a resistive sensor designed to measure angular position.

Fig 3.25   Angular position sensor
(a) Principle   (b) Construction

Capacitive types

The capacitive fluid level system has many advantages, not the least it is totally solid state, having no moving parts. Two electrically insulated tubes or probes act as the plates of the capacitor, and the operating principle is based on the difference between the dielectric constants of the fluid and of air. When the liquid is at the full level the capacitance element is covered and the fluid forms

the dielectric material and the sensor will give a 'full' capacitive reading.

When the fluid is below this level, the capacitance element will be partially or totally uncovered and surrounded in part or total by air, so producing a change in capacitance. Fig 3.26 shows the construction of such a sensor.

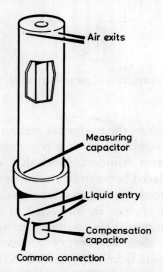

Fig 3.26   *Capacitive level sensor. Capacitance is proportional to the level of the fluid*

AC impedance type

This type of sensor relies on the conductivity of the fluid whose level is being measured. An AC signal is transmitted between a transmitter and receiver in the sensor, so that the received signal amplitude is a measure of fluid level. Fig 3.27 shows construction. Service checks should ensure that the resistance of the fluid does not change substantially due to additives or contaminants and so give false signals.

Hot wire type

The application of an electric current to a hot wire heating element produces a temperature rise dependent upon the heat dissipation into the surrounding medium, fluid or air. When covered by fluid, maximum heat dissipation occurs so that the

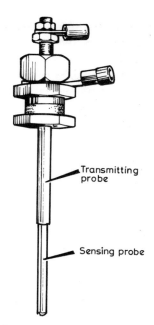

Fig 3.27   AC impedance level sensor

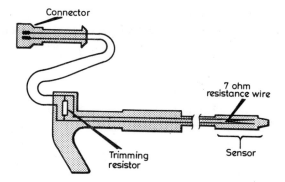

Fig 3.28   Typical oil level (dipstick) sensor

wire is at its lowest temperature and resistance. When not covered by fluid, heat dissipation is reduced and the wire is at a higher temperature and higher resistance value. Sensor details are shown in Fig 3.28. Hot wire sensors are most commonly used for engine oil monitoring, where a short application of current, immediately upon turning the engine on, indicates whether sufficient oil is present. Service checks should take into account the following factors:

1   the switching point from high to low levels is dependent upon temperature of the wire

2   the switching point may also be affected by the moisture content of the oil and deposits on the sensor

3   accurate monitoring also depends upon low resistance cables and terminal connections.

Reed switched type

In this type of sensor a permanent magnet is fixed to a fluid operated float. The reed switching contacts are embodied in the fixed part of the sensor body, so that a variable reluctance air gap is created and controlled by the level of the fluid. When the system is full the magnet will be in close proximity to the reed switch applying a strong magnetic field to close and hold the contacts closed. As the fluid level falls the air gap increases reducing the strength of the magnetic field on the reed, until it switches to the open position and provides the low level output signal. Fig 3.29 illustrates a typical sensor used for fluid level sensing in windscreen washer tanks.

In the body of the sensor are two resistors, connected in such a way that when the switch is closed (float up) the resistance between the pins in the connector is 180 ohms and when the switch

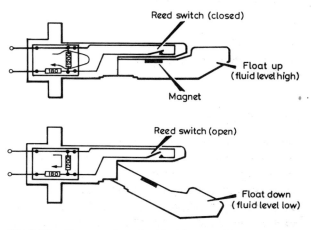

Fig 3.29   Construction of typical low wash/coolant fluid level sensor using float and reed switch principle

is open (float down) the resistance is 1380 ohms. One pin in the connector is earthed to the vehicle body locally via the wiring harness, the other is taken to the control assembly input.

For low screenwash, the switch operates with about one quarter of the fluid left in the container. For low coolant, the switch operates when the level in the overflow container is just below minimum.

4

Actuators

Actuators are the devices in a control system which convert an electrical input to a mechanical action. They provide a controllable force under command of the control unit. There are two basic types — solenoids and motors.

Solenoid

The solenoid is an electromagnetic device that produces a linear (straight line) mechanical force. The input signal produces a current flow in the solenoid coil, which in turn creates a strong magnetic field within and around the coil. This magnetic field applies an attractive force to the metal armature, pulling the armature into the centre of the coil. A spring forces the armature back out when the input signal is removed.

Fig 4.1(a) illustrates the operating principle of such a basic solenoid. Construction of a typical

plunger-type of solenoid is illustrated in Fig 4.1(b). Another type of solenoid, the flat-face type, is illustrated in Fig 4.1(c). Typical applications of solenoids in automotive systems are as fuel cut-off valves (Fig 4.1(d)) or fuel injector valves (Fig 4.1(e)).

The main disadvantage of the solenoid is due to the fact that the force produced by the linear movement is proportional to the square of the

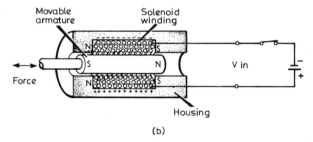

(b)

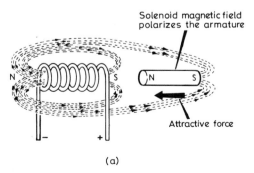

(a)

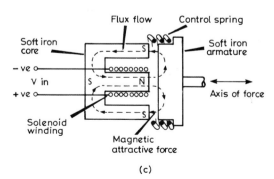

(c)

Fig 4.1   Solenoid actuator
(*a*) *Principle*

(*b*) *Plunger-type solenoid cross-sectional construction*
(*c*) *Flat face-type cross-sectional construction*

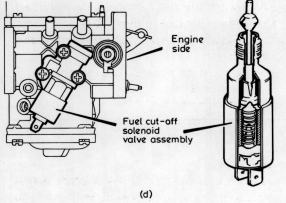

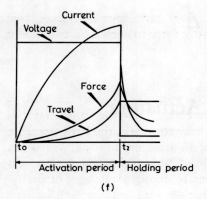

(d)

(f)

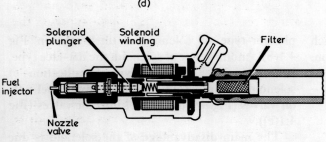

(e)

(d) *Fuel cut-off solenoid valve*
(e) *Cross-section of fuel injector valve*
(f) *Solenoid characteristics*

distance between the core and the magnetic pole piece. This limits solenoid use to applications requiring stroke distances of not more than 8 mm or so. Another disadvantage is the time taken for the solenoid to operate – the activation period. Both disadvantages are illustrated in Fig 4.1(f).

Service checks should ensure that all operating lengths and gaps are within the specifications, as well as the electrical factors.

Relays

A relay is an important part of many electrical control systems because it is an indirectly operated electrical switch that is useful for remote control and to control high current devices with a low current control signal.

The relay is basically a solenoid with a fixed core, in which the magnetic force is used to pull down an armature towards the core, and through the use of mechanical levers force electrical contacts to close. When the coil is demagnetised a return spring opens the contacts (Fig 4.2).

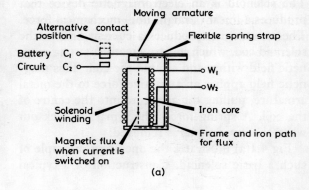

(a)

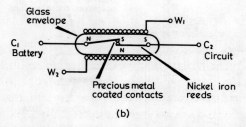

(b)

Fig 4.2   Two types of magnetic relays, using the solenoid principle
(a) *Basic relay in cross-section*
(b) *Cross-section of reed relay*

Some relays have normally closed contacts – the magnetic force in such devices opens them.

Electric motors

The electric motor is probably the most versatile of all actuators used in automotive control systems. Like solenoids, the basic operating principle is of an armature moving, owing to a magnetic field. Unlike solenoids, whose armatures move linearly, motor armatures generally rotate. . When coupled with low cost solid state control electronics a wide variety of motor-controlled proportional actuators are possible. In practice there are a number of different motor types that are commonly used in actuating systems.

DC motors

The basic DC motor construction is shown in Fig 4.3. All motors work on the basic magnet principle that like poles repel and opposites attract. In the case of the DC motor a main stationary magnetic field is produced by two permanent magnetic pole pieces. Another magnetic field is produced around a current-carrying armature winding. The two

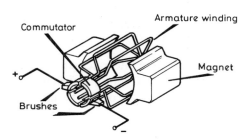

Fig 4.3 Basic structure of a DC motor. Armature shaft used to activate control mechanisms

magnetic field systems oppose each other resulting in a force being exerted on the armature, causing the armature to rotate. In order that the armature's magnetic field is always in the correct direction to maintain armature rotation, a commutator and brushes arrangement, illustrated in Fig 4.3, is used to switch the direction of armature current during rotation. DC motors can be made in a very wide

range of powers. For this discussion, however, we will look only at motors of about 100–150 watts, which include the majority of instrumentation and servo applications.

There are three main types of DC motors:
1   Iron-cored
2   Ironless rotor
3   Printed circuit.

Iron-cored motor
This is the traditional type of motor construction in which copper wire is wound onto an iron armature. The iron armature both supports the armature coil and concentrates the magnetic field created by passing current through the coil. The permanent field magnets are located around the circumference of the motor, and commutation is by carbon brushes onto a copper commutator. These motors are most commonly used in drive rather than servo applications. Fig 4.4 shows an iron-cored DC motor whose field magnet is, in fact, created by a coil.

Ironless rotor (coreless) motor
In this type of motor a central cylindrical permanent magnet is used around which a cylindrical coil of wire rotates. High grade precious metals are used in the brushes and commutators to mimimise contact resistance and friction. With no iron in the rotor there is low inertia, high efficiency, good performance-to-weight ratio and excellent servo characteristics.

Printed circuit motor
These motors comprise a disc of insulating material onto which a circuit of resistive conductors is printed. Carbon brushes contact with these conductors, and pass the current to create a magnetic field which interacts with radially placed permanent magnets. The printed disc has as many commutator bars as conductors to give a very smooth rotation, and no torque variation during its revolution. These motors create very good medium- to high-power drive and servo motors.

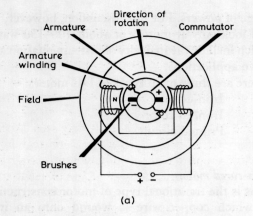

(a)

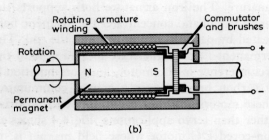

(b)

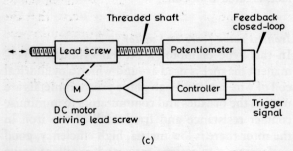

(c)

Fig 4.4   Typical types of DC motors
(a) Iron-cored motor
(b) Ironless motor
(c) DC servo motor system

DC servo motors

The servo motor makes use of a variable DC voltage for speed control. A potentiometer driven by the motor provides speed and position feedback to form a self-contained positioning system. An example is shown in Fig 4.4(c). These motors are used where precise position control is necessary along with high-speed operation.

Linear DC motors

The main disadvantage of conventional DC motors is that the speed of rotation has to be reduced and converted by a gearbox mechanism (Fig 4.5(a)) to provide a linear output. Fig 4.5(b)

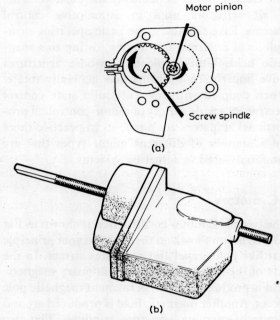

(a)

(b)

Fig 4.5   Linear DC motor actuators
(a) Greer mechanism
(b) Typical actuator

shows a small electric linear actuator which comprises a low voltage DC motor and short gear train driving a lead screw to provide the linear output, primarily designed for operating flaps in a heater or air conditioning unit.

One interesting development is the adaptation of a DC motor to provide linear motion directly, over a long stroke with a constant mechanical force. Fig 4.6 shows the operating principle of such a moving winding arrangement; in which the stationary centre core is a high flux permanent magnet and the moving winding is wound around the actuator piston assembly. When current is applied to the coil it creates a magnetic field system of the same polarity as the magnetic core. The two magnetic field systems interact, resulting in a force

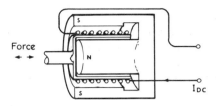

Fig 4.6   Moving winding linear DC motor

on the winding causing it to be expelled away from the stationary magnet in a linear direction.

Stepper motors

In a stepper motor many field windings are switched in rotation around a permanent magnet armature. The armature follows in small incremental steps. Fig 4.7 shows the basic operating principle of stepper motors, illustrated with mechanical switches to switch current to the field coils. In a practical stepper motor switching is electronic and digitally controlled. Rotational speed depends on how fast the magnetic field is incremented or rotated round the field system.

Stepper motors have a good stability and also

good torque when no power is applied, though the torque characteristic may be a limitation because it is inversely proportional to speed. If the motor is switched instantly from stop to full speed it will stall, therefore speed must be progressively increased. One other characteristic to bear in mind is their resonance point – at a low speed when the torque is drastically reduced it may stall. Also, a special driver unit is required with two input terminals; one to receive the driver pulse train and the other to designate the direction of rotation.

The most common type of stepper motors in automotive use have four phases giving five connections, one common positive supply and four negative returns. The electronic control unit earths combination of the returns causing the rotor to rotate in 7.5° (48 steps/rev) steps with up to some 150 combinations depending on the number of revolutions made by the rotor. A motor working on 48 pulses to rotate the spindle through one revolution requires 96 pulses per second to operate at a speed of 120 rev/min.

Output movement from a stepper motor can be rotary or linear, and it is often the case that the motor is not required to run at the optimum speed and torque. In which case a gearbox is used to modify the motor performance to match the load requirements, and/or convert the rotary action to a linear one.

Rotary solenoids (torque motor)

This type of solenoid actuator is used to provide rotational motion instead of linear motion.

Fig 4.8 shows the basic structure of torque motor which has two windings, which during an actuation period are loaded alternatively with voltages to exert opposing forces on the free rotating armature. By virtue of the armature's inertia the armature rotates to an angle directly corresponding to the ratio of the voltages applied to the two windings. It is the ability of this type of solenoid to combine large torque capability with very fast response times that make it suitable in many automotive control applications.

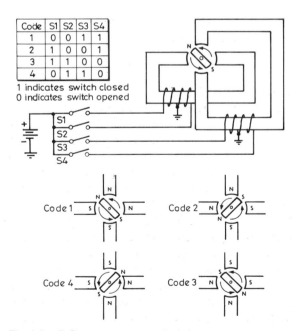

Fig 4.7   DC stepper motor principle

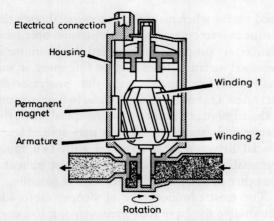

Fig 4.8   Rotary solenoid actuator (torque motor)

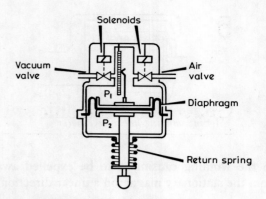

Fig 4.9   Typical electro-pneumatic actuator

Electro-pneumatic actuator

This type of actuator is a vacuum operated dia-phragm device, which can move against a return spring. The operating pressure (atmospheric and/or partial vacuum in the inlet manifold) is controlled by solenoid operated valve(s) which regulate the pressure difference either side of the diaphragm, so producing a linear movement. Fig 4.9 outlines the operating principles of a typical electro-pneumatic actuator.

5

Generator electronic systems

The satisfactory performance of a vehicle's electrical and electronic components depends to a certain extent on a reliable and constantly available supply of power. It is the task of the generator and its associated control electronics to provide the on-board electrical power to supply loads and for storage in the battery. Fig 5.1 shows in block diagram form the generator system.

Generation

Fig 5.2(a) illustrates the principle of AC single phase generation. Typically, vehicle alternators use three sets of output windings, spaced at 120° intervals around the armature (Fig 5.2(b)) so that the rotating magnetic field cuts through three fields and each output winding produces an AC

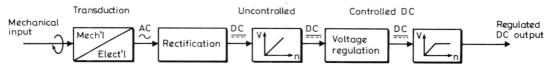

Fig 5.1   Block diagram of a generator system

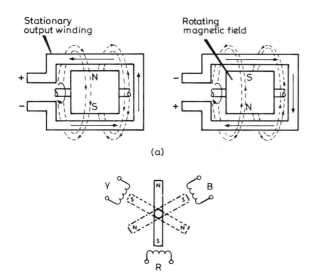

(a)

(b)

(c)

Fig 5.2   Alternator voltage generation principles
(a)   Simplified single phase alternator. In practice an electromagnetic field system is used rather than a permanent magnet
(b)   Arrangement of output windings in a three phase alternator
(c)   Voltage curves over one revolution of rotating magnet. Connection of the windings results in a three phase alternating voltage

output. The voltage waveforms of such a three-phase alternator are illustrated in Fig 5.2(c). To minimise the number of output terminals the three windings are connected in either star or delta formations (Fig 5.3).

In the star connection method the amplitudes of the total generated output voltage and any one phase voltage differ by the factor $\sqrt{3}{:}1$ (i.e. 1.73:1). The output current amplitude however, equals the amplitude of any one phase current. Conversely, in the delta connection method the amplitude of the output voltage equals the amplitude of any phase voltage but the output current is $\sqrt{3}$ times one phase current.

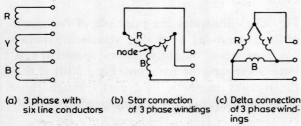

(a) 3 phase with six line conductors (b) Star connection of 3 phase windings (c) Delta connection of 3 phase windings

Fig 5.3   Alternator starter winding connections

Rectification

Conversion from AC to DC is known as rectification and is done with semiconductor diodes. Fig 5.4 shows how a single diode allows the positive half cycle of an alternating current wave to pass through but blocks the negative half cycle,

giving rise to this configuration's name: half-wave rectifier.

A more efficient method uses two diodes to give full wave rectification, in which both half cycles are rectified. Use is made of an output winding with a centre tap to achieve this. During positive half cycles (Fig 5.5(a)) diode D_1 conducts; during negative half cycles (Fig 5.5(b)) diode D_2 conducts. The resultant waveform is shown in Fig 5.5(c).

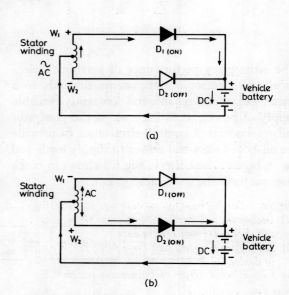

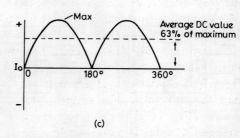

Fig 5.5   Full wave rectification of a single phase alternating current
(a) *Positive half cycle from W1 conducted by diode D1: Diode D2 not conducting due to negative bias at W2. First half cycle passed through to the battery*
(b) *Second half cycle finds W2 positive and diode D2 conducts current to battery while diode D1 is negatively biased and is off*
(c) *Single phase full wave rectification output wave form*

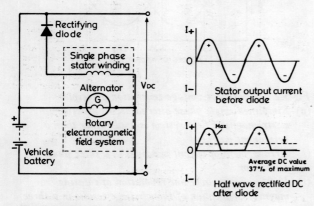

Fig 5.4   Single phase half wave rectification

Another method of full-wave rectification uses a bridge rectifier, without a tapped output winding (Fig 5.6). During positive half cycles diodes D_1 and D_3 conduct, while during negative half cycles diodes D_2 and D_4 conduct.

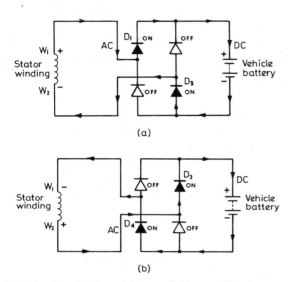

(a)

(b)

Fig 5.6   Single phase full wave bridge rectification
(a) During the positive half cycle point W1 is positive and diodes D1 and D4 conduct
(b) During the negative half cycle point W2 is positive so diodes D2 and D4 conduct

Bridge rectification can be used with a three-phase alternator, as shown in Fig 5.7(a), to give DC output. During each half cycle of each phase three diodes conduct, so the output waveform of a three-phase full wave rectifier comprises six positive half cycles per revolution, as shown in Fig 5.7(b). As the waveform is much smoother than the waveform of a single phase full wave rectifier (Fig. 5.6(c)) it can be appreciated that the average DC value is correspondingly greater.

An electromagnetic field system is used in automotive alternators and the excitation current is tapped from the three-phase alternator output in a process known as self-excitation. A separate diode circuit (auxiliary field diodes) is used to rectify the excitation field current. Fig 5.8 shows a typical circuit.

The rectifier diodes in the alternator not only

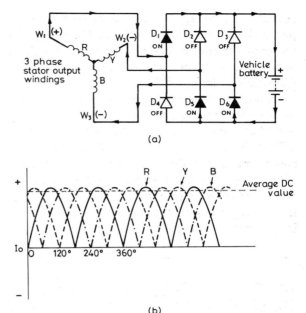

(a)

(b)

Fig 5.7   Three phase alternator and full wave bridge rectifier
(a) Positive half cycle of first phase
(b) Output waveform comprising six half cycles per revolution

rectify the excitation current and the generator current, but they also prevent the battery from discharging through the three-phase stator windings when the engine is stopped or the operating

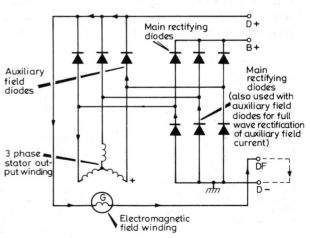

Fig 5.8   Rectification of self-excited electromagnetic rotor field current

speed is so low that the output voltage is less than battery voltage. Current can only flow from the alternator to the battery and not vice versa. The silicon diodes block the current against a voltage of up to approximately 350–400 volts. If this breakdown voltage were exceeded the diodes would be destroyed by the high breakdown current.

Voltage drop across the main diodes in operation causes a power loss which is dissipated in the form of heat. Power diodes (25W) are used for this reason and they are mounted on heat sinks to aid cooling. Care must be taken not to reverse battery polarity otherwise a short circuit is created through the power diodes and the excessive current flow could destroy them. The auxiliary field exciter diodes carry a relatively small current hence the exciter diodes are smaller and need dissipate only about 1W.

Filtering

The output waveform of the three-phase full wave rectifier is fairly smooth in appearance and the average DC value closely approaches the optimum. Further smoothing can be effected by filtering, and capacitive and/or inductive circuits may be used for this purpose. In automotive systems the battery creates an inherent smoothing effect; as current is supplied from the battery into the system during times when the rectifier output would otherwise be below the battery voltage.

During times when the rectifier output is above battery voltage the battery is recharged. A possible smoothed DC voltage is shown in Fig 5.9. The amount with which the output varies above and below the optimum is called the ripple voltage.

Voltage regulation

The voltage generated by an alternator increases as its rotational speed increases, and also as the strength of the excitation field current increases. At about 10,000 rev/min the open circuit voltage on full excitation current (2A) could be as high as 140 volts, which is far too high for an automotive system. The principle of voltage regulation consists of varying the value of the auxiliary field excitation current in a way which maintains a working voltage of approximately 14 volts, i.e. sufficiently high to provide power for all the vehicle's electrical systems and recharge the battery, but not too high to cause damage. The voltage regulator is designed to reduce the field current as the stator voltage output increases thus preventing the output voltage exceeding the safe working limit of around 14 volts. As long as the alternator and rectifier's output voltage remains below the working limit, the electronic regulator is not in operation. When the voltage exceeds 14 volts the regulator automatically reduces the output voltage, depending on the load on the alternator, by interrupting the excitation current. The magnetic field strength of the rotor decreases

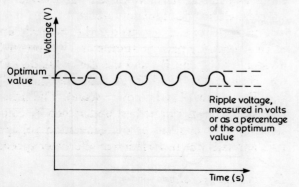

Fig 5.9   A smoothed DC voltage, such as may be derived from an automotive generating system

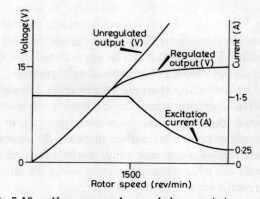

Fig 5.10   Alternator and control characteristics

and so does the output voltage. Fig 5.10 shows typical alternator and control characteristics.

When the voltage drops below a pre-set minimum the excitation current is increased again, and the output voltage rises until the maximum voltage is exceeded again. This switching cycle takes place automatically and at a frequency that ensures the output voltage is regulated to the desired mean value. At low speeds the excitation current flows for a relatively long period of time, so that its mean value is high (1.5A). At high speeds the excitation current flows only briefly, hence the mean value is low (0.25A). Fig 5.11 shows possible

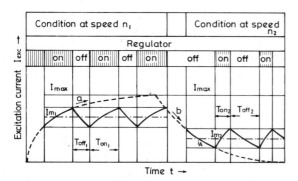

Fig 5.11   Excitation current I_{exc} as a function of on time T_{on} and off-time T_{off}. The relationship between on-time and off-time is decisive with regard to the magnitude of the resulting mean excitation current I_m. The excitation current rises along curve a and decays (decay current i_A) along curve b. The graph is intended to convey a general impression only. The values shown are not in accordance with actual values.

switching characteristics of the excitation current and its mean values.

Throughout this high speed switching process the field winding represents a high inductive load, and so the excitation current does not undergo abrupt changes – due to self-induction. Output current may be self-limiting as the output winding reaction limits the maximum current flow at full load, so at high speeds a weak magnetic flux is sufficient for generating the necessary output voltage.

Electronic regulators

The advantages of the electronic regulator are so significant that it has become an item of standard equipment. The electronic regulator is usually small enough to be alternator-mounted: Body-mounted regulators are now only used with alternators having high excitation currents or where special requirements are demanded.

The most important electronic components in the regulator are transistors and a Zener diode. The transistor has the function of switching the

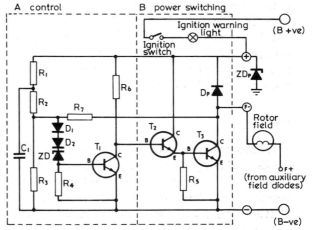

Fig 5.12   Electronic voltage regulator. Circuit diagram

field excitation current on and off while the Zener diode is used for controlling the transistors by acting as a voltage sensitive switch. Fig 5.12 shows a typical electronic regulator circuit.

The regulator can be considered to be made up of two parts (1) part A: transistor T_1, potential divider R_1, R_2, and R_3, and the Zener Diode ZD (the control stage) and (2) Part B: transistors T_2 and T_3, resistor R_5 (the power stage). The principle of operation can be best understood by considering what happens as the generation voltage rises and falls due to variation in alternator speed.

Low voltage operation
Whenever the actual output voltage is below the maximum preset generator voltage, no current

flows to the Zener diode and so no base current is supplied to transistor T_1 which is therefore in the non-conducting state (switched off). With transistor T_1 off, control current flows from the positive (+ ve) terminal via resistor R_6 to the base of transistor T_2, switching the transistor on. This in turn, supplies base current to power transistor T_3, switching it, too, on. Transistors T_2 and T_3 form a circuit known as a Darlington pair – a high power gain amplifying circuit. With transistor T_3 on, field excitation current flows through the field windings and the transistor, causing the generated output voltage to rise.

High voltage operation

When the generated output voltage exceeds the working limit (14V), the breakdown voltage of Zener diode ZD is also exceeded, and so the Zener diode conducts. Control current now flows via resistors R_1 and R_2, and the diodes D_1 and D_2, to the base of transistor T_1, switching T_1 on. The base voltage of transistor T_2 drops below 0.6V and so base current stops flowing, resulting in the transistor pair being switched off. With transistor T_3 off no field excitation current flows and so the generated output voltage falls again.

These cycles are repeated continuously switching the field excitation current on and off to regulate the generated output voltage to around 14V. The ratio of on to off times of the excitation current depends upon the rotational speed of the engine and the electrical load requirements.

To aid stability, resistor R_1 and capacitor C_1 form a filter which smooths the generated voltage. Diodes D_1 and D_2 act as temperature compensating elements to ensure that the output voltage is not only temperature stable, but is slightly reduced during the hot summer periods and increased in winter. This is useful to counteract the higher operating current drain on the battery in the cold, dark months. At the instant power transistor T_3 switches off, a large voltage spike is generated in the rotor field winding due to self-induction as the field current is interrupted. This self-induced voltage spike might damage the transistor, so to provide effective protection a pro-

tection diode D_p, is connected in parallel with the rotor field excitation winding, allowing decay of residual current whenever a voltage spike occurs. The self-induced voltage spikes are of a higher potential than the generated output voltage and so diode D_p conducts as they occur, dissipating their energy as heat.

Additional protection is also usually provided against overvoltage which may occur as a result of: regulator failure; switching off of high inductive loads; loose contacts; or breaks in conductor cables. A Zener diode ZD_p, is often used as a protective device, reverse biased between the battery positive (B +) terminal and earth. The breakdown voltage of this Zener diode is typically between 20 and 30 volts and provides adequate protection for rated outputs up to 35A. Whenever an overvoltage condition exists the Zener diode conducts and current flows through to earth, protecting the regulator.

This operating principle is basically the same for all types of alternator electronic regulators, though they may look different in appearance and circuit layout.

Hybrid voltage regulator (Fig 5.13)

The current trend is towards the use of integrated circuit regulators, comprising a hybrid IC with built in monolithic integrated circuits (MIC). The basic principle of operation is still the same, whereby the MIC detects the alternator output voltage and, by switching transistors on and off, controls the current in the field windings, maintaining the alternator output voltage at a constant level.

Operation

When the ignition is switched on, without the engine running, battery voltage is applied to the IC, and transistor T1 is on. Current flows through the field winding circuit via T1 to earth, exciting the field windings. In this condition (i.e. the alternator is not turning) the phase voltage at terminal

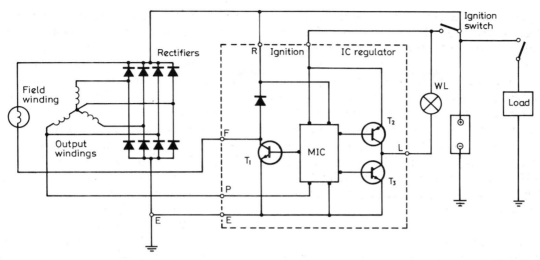

Fig. 5.13   Hybrid–monolithic IC voltage regulation

P is zero (0V), and the IC turns on transistor T3 which completes an earth path for charge warning lamp.

Once the engine is running and the alternator generates current the phase voltage at terminal P increases. The IC senses this increase in voltage and switches T3 off and transistor T2 on, applying a positive potential to the warning lamp, so the lamp goes out.

The alternator output voltage is sensed, at terminal B, by the IC. When the voltage exceeds 14V the IC switches transistor T1 off, switching off the exciting current to the field winding. When the alternator voltage falls below 14V the IC switches transistor T1 on again, allowing the field current to flow through the field winding once more. This cycle continues maintaining a regulated output voltage of 14V.

6

Electronic ignition systems

The function of the ignition system is to ignite the compressed air and fuel mixture, at the correct time, and initiate its combustion. In the spark ignition engine this is achieved by means of brief electrical arc discharge (a spark) between the electrodes of the sparking plug. The energy required to ignite an air-fuel ratio of 14.7:1 by means of an electrical spark is approximately 0.2 MJ. Richer and leaner mixture ratios may require more than 3 MJ. If the ignition energy available is insufficient then ignition will not occur, the mixture cannot ignite and combustion will not take place.

A spark can arc from one electrode to the other only when a sufficiently high voltage is present to make the gap between the electrodes become electrically conductive. Under the high cylinder pressure conditions of a typical IC petrol engine the ignition voltage may need to be as high as 5 K to 20 KV, depending upon the type of engine and spark plug. There is also the need for the voltage at the plug electrodes to increase rapidly from zero until the spark discharge voltage is reached and for the spark voltage to be maintained for a suitable duration to ensure that the air-fuel mixture can wholly ignite.

Ever since 1908 when Charles F. Kettering patented his battery ignition system most vehicles have had this conventional electromagnetic inductive system (the Kettering ignition system) fitted as standard. As you can see from Fig 6.1 the system has a number of functions to perform, and several components are used in doing so. Let's

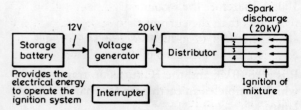

Fig 6.1   Block diagram of battery ignition system

begin with the high voltage generation and energy storage.

In battery ignition systems the voltage required for spark ignition is created by means of an electromagnetic induction coil (the ignition coil). The coil is used to step the voltage from the battery (12 volts in most vehicles) up to ignition voltage (5,000 to 20,000 volts). The ignition coil is, in effect, a transformer, made up of two separate windings called the primary and secondary windings, both wound around the same laminated iron core. The secondary winding has many more turns than the primary winding. It is the ratio of turns in the primary and secondary windings which determines the increase in voltage achieved. If the secondary winding has 100 times the number of turns wound on the primary windings (a typical value), the secondary voltage will be 100 times greater than the primary voltage (assuming 100% efficiency), according to the equation:

$$\frac{V2}{V1} = \frac{N2}{N1}$$

where V2 = secondary voltage; V1 = primary voltage; N2 = secondary turns; N1 = primary turns.

Rearranging, the secondary voltage is given by:

$$V2 = \frac{N2 \times V1}{N1}$$

This stepping up of voltage is done at the expense of the strength of the sparks, because proportional to the increase in voltage induced in the secondary winding there is a decrease in the value of the secondary current. The secondary current is in fact, reduced by the same factor (in our example 100:1), therefore the secondary current will be 100 times less than the current flowing in the primary at the moment of induction. For this reason the diameter of the wire used in the secondary winding is thinner than that of the primary.

The final value of the stepped up secondary voltage is also influenced by:

1   the rate of change of the magnetic field
2   the strength of the magnetic field current.

The conventional (Kettering) ignition system and more modern electronic ignition systems generate the ignition voltage in the same way. In the interval (dwell period) between two sparks, energy is stored in the ignition coil. The energy is stored as a magnetic field in the soft iron-core of the coil, created by the current flowing through the coil primary winding when connected to the battery supply. When the primary current flow is interrupted the magnetic field rapidly breaks down and its energy is returned to the coil as an induced voltage. As both primary and secondary windings are surrounded by the magnetic field a voltage will be induced into both: the primary induced voltage is approximately 150–300 volts but the secondary induced voltage is 100 times greater i.e. 15,000 to 30,000 volts. The high secondary voltage is sufficient to force a current to flow through the air gap between the spark plug electrodes, in the form of a spark.

On the other hand, the rate at which the magnetic field builds up when the primary circuit is connected to the battery is relatively slow; with

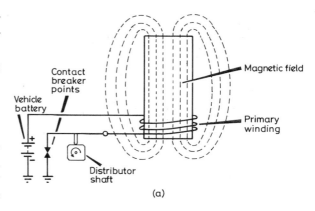

(a)

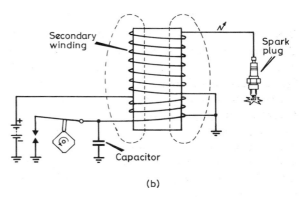

(b)

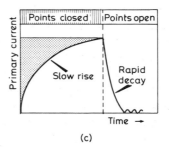

(c)

Fig 6.2   Illustrating the Kettering ignition system

(a) *Inductive energy is stored as a magnetic field, set-up by the current flowing in the primary winding when the contact breaker points are closed*

(b) *Primary current is cut-off as the points are opened and so the magnetic field breaks down, returning the energy stored to the primary winding as a high induced voltage. A capacitor speeds up field breakdown and helps prevent arcing at the points. The high primary voltage creates a higher secondary voltage, sufficient to generate a spark*

(c) *Showing the difference in rise and decay times of primary current*

the result that the induced secondary voltage during this time is below the required spark ignition voltage and no spark occurs. From this it can be seen that the secondary voltage is not directly related to the 12 volt supply, but is more dependent on the speed at which the magnetic field is switched. This basic principle of operation of the Kettering battery ignition system is illustrated in Fig 6.2.

The ignition energy, high voltage and speed of operation of the Kettering battery ignition system are limited mainly by the electrical and mechanical switching capacity of the contact breaker points. In electronic ignition systems, however, the contact breaker points are replaced by non-contacting, non-wearing signal generators and electronic power switches, with most other parts of the Kettering system retained. Typically, therefore, an electronic ignition system is made up of:

1   an ignition coil
2   a distributor; in which the distributor cap, rotor, and advance/retard mechanism work exactly as in the conventional Kettering system.
3   an electronic switch
4   ignition cables and spark plugs. Fig 6.3 illustrates such a system. The ignition coil used in many electronic ignition systems has a low impedence primary winding, to reduce inductance and thus improve coil performance – this has been done simply by reducing the number of turns on the primary winding, which, in turn, increases the winding ratio to around 250–300:1. To limit the primary current a ballast resistor is added.

The ballast resistor (0.65 ohm) also prevents overheating and provides thermal adjustment. From cold the resistance is low, therefore the primary current and secondary voltage is high. During idling the resistor heats up, resistance increases and the primary current is reduced. At high engine speeds, the amount of time the primary circuit is closed is very short, so heating of the resistor is limited and the primary current remains high. When the starter motor is operated

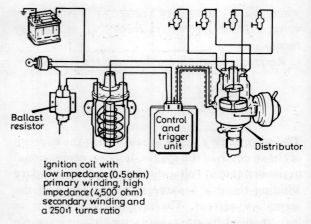

Ignition coil with low impedance(0.5ohm) primary winding, high impedance(4,500 ohm) secondary winding and a 250:1 turns ratio

Fig 6.3   Basic electronic ignition system – without contact breaker points

the ballast resistor is by-passed, in order to compensate for the voltage drop when the high starting current is drawn from the battery and thus provide the best conditions for starting.

From this basic electronic ignition system several others have evolved and are now in common use. The remainder of this chapter is devoted to explaining their principles of operations. All rely on the principle that the mechanical contact breaker points are replaced by a signal generator. The function of the signal generator is merely to generate signals corresponding to the positions of the pistons and feed them to a control unit. To this end, the signal generator may be housed in the distributor (as the contact breaker points of the Kettering system are) or any other place where information regarding piston position can be derived, e.g. directly from the flywheel or the camshaft. In the control unit the signals are conditioned to create a control waveform of sufficient magnitude to trigger the power switching transistor. This, in turn, triggers the ignition spark voltage in synchronism with the trigger signal pulses. The distributor assembly connects the coil's secondary voltage to the spark plugs in the correct timing sequence.

The control signal voltage can be generated in various ways, the most common being:

1   magnetic reluctance

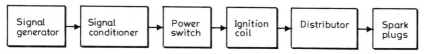

Fig 6.4   Block diagram of a basic electronic ignition system, followed by most systems available

2   photo–electric effect
3   Hall effect

Fig 6.4 shows a block diagram of an electronic ignition system. Virtually all electronic ignition systems follow this simple format, in which a spark is created as the direct result of a signal from the signal generator. A signal conditioner shapes and amplifies the signal from the signal generator to a level where it is capable of driving a power switch (generally a transistor) which turns on and off current in the ignition coil's primary winding. We shall now consider electronic ignition systems with a number of signal generation methods.

Electronic coil ignition system with magnetic reluctor signal generator

As the name implies this system uses a variable reluctance magnetic generator. When a reluctor tooth passes the magnetic core of an inductive coil winding the magnetic field strength intensifies. The changing magnetic flux induces a voltage in the pick-up coil winding.

Fig 6.5 shows this induction process in greater detail. As the reluctor tooth approaches the pick-up assembly the air gap is progressively reduced, reducing the reluctance of the air gap to the flow of magnetic flux from the permanent magnet. As the air gap's reluctance decreases the flow of magnetic flux increases inducing a voltage into the winding, as the magnetic flux builds up from zero to a maximum value. When the tooth is directly opposite the pick-up assembly the flux is at a maximum value and the induced voltage reaches its maximum value. As the 'tooth' rotates away from the pick-up and the gap increases the magnetic flux changes from a maximum value to a minimum value and the induced voltage is of the opposite polarity. The frequency with which the pulsed induced voltage occurs is proportional to

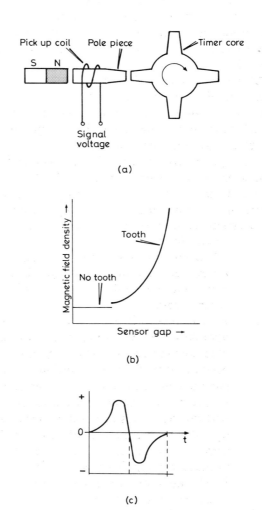

Fig 6.5   Magnetic reluctor signal generator

engine speed and the number of cylinders in the engine.

Electronic control

The induced signal is fed to the electronic control unit via a two core cable. In the control unit there

..., one that receives the signal ... the signal generator, amplifies and changes ... so that it can control the other main part. The power switching transistors. The control circuit also incorporates electronic devices for varying the dwell period. Fig 6.6 shows in block diagram form the functional units of the electronic control unit.

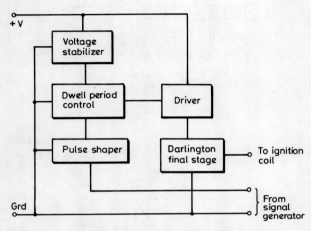

Fig 6.6   Block diagram of electronic control unit

Pulse shaping

The pulse shaper is a Schmitt trigger, which converts the signal pulse into a square waveform (Fig 6.7). The signal is applied via terminals 1 and 2.

Initially current from the positive supply rail

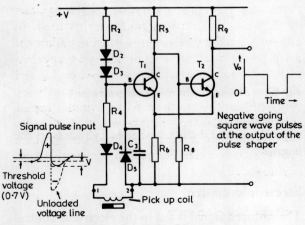

Fig 6.7   Schmitt trigger pulse Shaper

reaches the base of transistor T_1 via resistor R_2, and diodes D_2 and D_3, switching T_1 on which, in turn holds transistor T_2 off. The output voltage of the pulse shaper circuit is therefore high. The positive part of the signal pulse is blocked by diode D_4, so transistor T_1 (and the rest of the circuit) is unaffected. The negative part of the signal pulse, however, reduces the base voltage of transistor T_1. When the base voltage reduces below the threshold voltage of the transistor (0.7V) the transistor turns off, turning transistor T_2 on and the output voltage goes low. When the negative part of the signal pulse decays, the base voltage of T_1 again increases above the threshold voltage and the transistor once more turns on, turning T_2 off, and the output goes high. Thus, the pulse shaper action is to create a train of negative-going square wave pulses in synchronism with each signal pulse.

Diode D_5 prevents large negative signal pulse voltages damaging T_1 by turning on and simply short circuiting the signal pulse if the base voltage of T_1 falls below -0.7V. Diodes D_2 and D_3 act as temperature compensating elements.

Dwell period control

The dwell period control ensures that sufficient energy is stored in the ignition coil for spark generation under all engine operating conditions, including high engine speeds.

Fig 6.8 illustrates the two switching states of the dwell period control. Capacitor C_5 and resistors R_9 and R_{11} serve as a simple RC network to vary the time transistor T_3 conducts and hence the dwell period. Consider transistor T_2 just turning off (Fig 6.8(a)): capacitor C_5 charges via R_9 and the base-emitter circuit of transistor T_3. At low engine speeds there is sufficient time for C_5 to reach its fully charged state, with almost 12 V across it, during which transistor T_3 is switched on and conducts. When transistor T_2 is swiched on, at the point of ignition, C_5 discharges through R_{11} and T_2, applying a negative potential to the base of T_3 switching T_3 off. Once discharged, C_5 starts to re-charge in the opposite direction via R_{11} and T_2 so changing the polarity of the capacitor plates

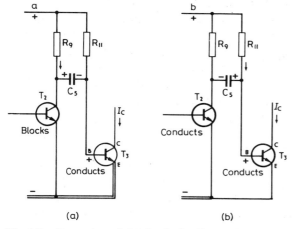

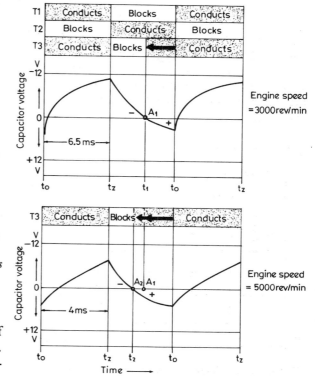

Fig 6.8   Operation of the simple dwell period control in two switching states (a) Charging of the capacitor (b) Charge reversal of the capacitor – as the capacitor plates change polarity, transistor T_3 once again turns on and conducts

Fig 6.9   Showing the variable dwell period of two different engine speeds. At higher speeds the capacitor does not have as much time in which to charge, so it reaches the point of polarity change (A_2) sooner than of lower speeds (A_1)

and applying a positive potential to the base of transistor T_3, switching T_3 on again (Fig 9.8(b)). Capacitor C_5 continues to charge up until transistor T_2 is switched off.

The action of transistor T_3 mirrors the action of the ignition coil primary windings' current-switching transistor, so when T_3 is on primary current is building up inside the ignition coil. When T_3 is switched off the primary current is switched off to produce the secondary ignition voltage.

The main feature of the dwell control is that transistor T_3 switches on as the plates of capacitor C_5 undergo a polarity change during the capacitor's recharge phase. The point in time at which the capacitor's plates change polarity depends upon the voltage to which the capacitor has been charged. As the engine speed increases the charging time of the capacitor decreases and the charge voltage must be lower and so the polarity change occurs more quickly, so beginning the start of the dwell period at a correspondingly earlier point. Fig 6.9 shows the variable dwell period and related capacitor voltages.

With six and eight cylinder engines at high speeds there is a danger that this simple dwell

control will reduce the time during which transistor T_3 is off (the pulse pause) to such an extent that a long enough spark to give reliable ignition of the air-fuel mixture is no longer ensured. In any situation the dwell control must not allow the pulse pause (spark period) to fall below approximately 0.5 ms and an additional capacitor, C_4, and Zener diode, ZD_2, are included in the network (Fig 6.10) for this purpose. At six cylinder engine speeds above 5000 rev/min the length of the pulse pause is constant, resulting in a dwell period which does not change significantly up to the maximum engine speed.

Voltage stabilization

As with all electronic devices, high performance

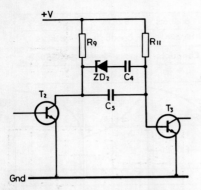

Fig 6.10 Enhanced dwell period control to maintain a constant dwell period at high engine speeds

is only possible when the supply voltage is stable. In this electronic ignition system this is the function of the following components, Zener diode ZD_1, capacitors C_1 and C_2 and resistor R_1. They are connected together as shown in Fig 6.11. The automotive supply voltage (V_B) can vary between about 8 and 15 volts. The voltage (V_s) to the control unit's electronic devices is reduced by the value of the voltage drop across R_1 caused by the flow of supply current (I_s).

$$V_s = V_B - I_s \times R_1$$

When the automotive supply voltage exceeds the required value Zener diode ZD_1 conducts causing a higher current flow through R_1, and thus an additional voltage drop across R_1, which reduces the overvoltage. In this way the voltage to the pulse shaper and dwell control remains constant,

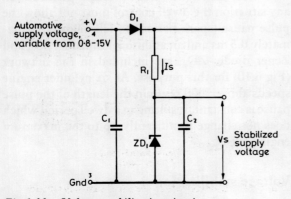

Fig 6.11 Voltage stabilisation circuit

regardless of the automotive supply voltage, at a level determined by the Zener diode. Capacitor C_2 is used to filter the ripple voltage present on the automotive supply while capacitor C_1 absorbs any induced voltage spikes coming from the rest of the vehicle's electrical system. In some electronic ignition systems the supply voltage is stabilised by using a simple RC network without a Zener diode.

Power switching

Final electronic power switching (Fig 6.12) is done by means of a Darlington pair transistor circuit T_5, T_6 which has a high input impedence (around 1 megohm), and produces very high current gain (typically several thousand). The Darlington pair is driven by transistors T_3 and T_4. When T_3 is off the base terminal of T_4 is positive, switching T_4

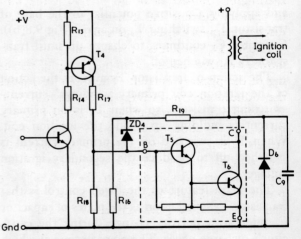

Fig 6.12 Darlington final switching stage

on. The flow of collector current through T_4 and the voltage divider R_{17} and R_{18} provides the base bias voltage for T_5. Transistor T_5 conducts, switching on T_6 and so the coil primary current flows through the Darlington pair. The magnetic field builds up in the ignition coil to provide the energy storage.

The primary current continues to flow until T_3 is switched on, which reduces the bias at the base

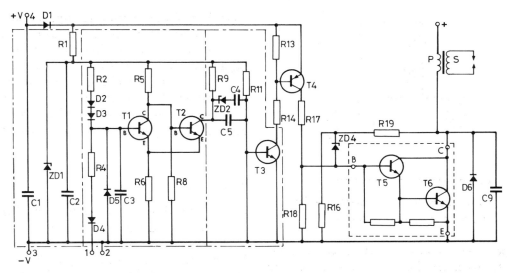

Fig 6.13   Complete circuit diagram of the electronic ignition system with magnetic reluctor signal generator

of T_4, turning T_4 off. In turn, this switches the Darlington transistors off to interrupt the flow of primary current and generate a high voltage discharge across a spark plug's electrodes.

Diode D_6 provides protection from self-induced voltage spikes caused by the rapid switching of the primary current. The diode dissipates the induced electrical energy in the form of heat. In addition further protection is offered by capacitor C_9, which short circuits to ground any oscillations due to the rapid switching. Capacitor C_9 also acts as an interference suppressor. Zener diode ZD_4 provides feedback to the base of T_5 to promote rapid switching and keep the transistor firmly switched on when activated.

The complete circuit of this electronic ignition system is shown in Fig 6.13. In commercial systems it is likely that most of the circuits discussed and shown here will be in an integrated circuit form. It is also possible that operational amplifier integrated circuits may be used for amplification and or the Schmitt trigger.

Electronic ignition system with Hall effect generator

The Hall generator assembly is located in the ignition distributor. It consists of 1) a stationary vane switch (the sensor) and; 2) a rotating vane assembly attached to the top of the distributor shaft (Fig 6.14). A permanent magnet provides the magnetic flux to activate the Hall chip and create the Hall voltage. The Hall voltage signal is generated by the vanes of the rotor passing through the air gap of the vane switch without making contact as the distributor shaft rotates. If the air gap is unobstructed the magnetic flux flows across the air gap, creating maximum Hall voltage. When a solid vane moves into the air gap it pro-

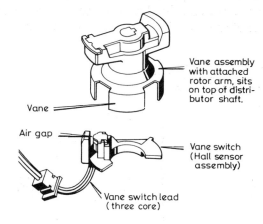

Fig 6.14   Components of the Hall signal generator assembly (within the distributor)

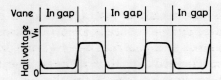

Fig 6.15   Signal generated by vanes cutting through the air gap of the Hall sensor assembly

vides a magnetic shunt which short circuits the magnet flux away from the Hall sensor and minimum Hall voltage is created. As the vane assembly rotates, therefore, a signal is created (Fig 6.15) of a negative-going pulse every time a vane cuts

through the sensor air gap. The widths of the vanes initially determine the dwell period and the number of vanes corresponds to the number of engine cylinders.

The Hall IC comprises a number of circuits which amplify and process the Hall signal voltage. A block diagram of the Hall IC is shown in Fig 6.16. Signal conditioning, it should be noted, is performed by the sensor assembly itself, and *not* in the main control circuit.

Electronic control unit

The electronic control unit (Fig 6.17) receives the

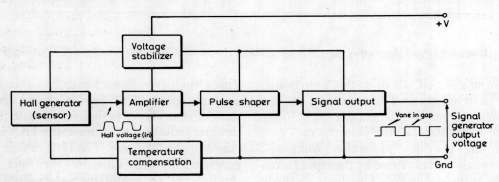

Fig 6.16   Block diagram of Hall IC

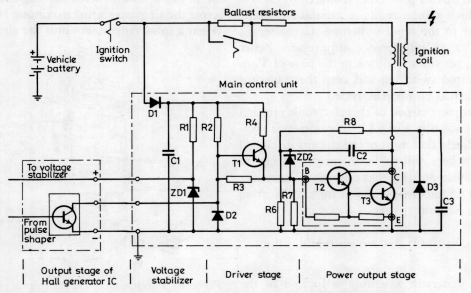

Fig 6.17   Circuit of electronic ignition system main control unit and peripheral components

sensor signal to produce the secondary voltage required for ignition purposes. When the Hall IC's output transistor is on its output voltage is about 0.4V i.e. below the value required to switch transistor T_1 on. No current flows through resistor R_7 to create the voltage drop required to turn on transistor T_2. The Darlington output stage is therefore off and no primary current flows.

When a vane enters the air gap of the vane switch, the Hall IC output transistor switches off, and the resultant high output voltage causes transistor T_1 to switch on. In this state the base of T_2 becomes positively biased and so the Darlington transistor pair turns on and primary current can now flow.

Constant energy ignition systems

Constant energy ignition systems are a variation of the two electronic ignition systems already discussed and, like them, use a variable reluctance magnetic, or Hall sensor signal generator along with a coil, distributor and control circuit. Main difference is that feedback systems are used in the control circuit which ensure the correct value of primary winding current flows through the coil under all engine operating conditions.

This feature means that: (1) the open circuit secondary output voltage is almost constant over a wide range of engine conditions; (2) the primary current is limited to a safe maximum value; (3) no ballast resistors are needed, as the coil primary current is varied automatically according to requirements.

Fig 6.18 shows a block diagram of a constant energy ignition system, using a magnetic reluctance signal generator. The pulsed signal (identical to that in Fig 6.5) is shaped by a pulse shaping circuit formed with an operational amplifier. The output of the pulse shaper switches the driver amplifier on and off which, in turn, switches the Darlington transistor pair output stage on and off, making and breaking the primary current to the coil. This operation is similar in principle to the control circuits of the two preceding electronic ignition systems.

A resistor is connected in series with the output stage and primary winding which is used as a current sensing resistor. Current flow through the resistor creates a voltage drop across it which is compared with a reference voltage by an operational amplifier comparator. The reference voltage is defined by the maximum current to be allowed through the primary winding (5.6 A) and

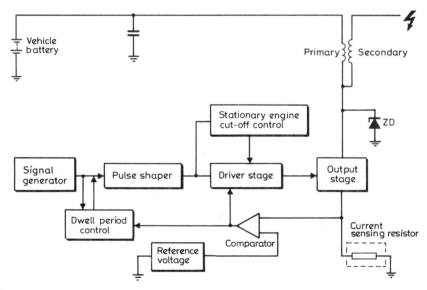

Fig 6.18   Block diagram of a constant energy electronic ignition system

the current sensing resistor value, according to Ohm's law:

$$V = IR$$

When the voltage drop equals the reference voltage the maximum current has been reached, and the comparator reduces the output of the driver stage, forcing the output stage off; thus reducing the primary current. This feedback loop ensures that the primary current limit of 5.6 A cannot be exceeded. The effect of the feedback loop is to vary the resistance of the output stage electronically, thus controlling the flow of primary current. The output stage resistance, according to Ohm's law, creates a voltage drop across it. During operation this voltage drop can take on various values; depending upon battery voltage and circuit temperature and load conditions. Approximately 6 to 8V is dropped across the output transistor during the actual current limiting period, and a great deal of heat would be dissipated if the situation were to remain for any great period of time. Fortunately, the dwell period control ensures that the time during which current limiting occurs is small and so average heat generation is not large.

The pulsed signal from the signal generator and

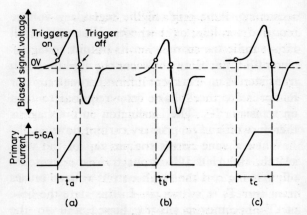

Fig 6.19   *Effects of varying the DC bias on the dwell period*

(*a*) *DC bias is correct; time t_a is sufficient to allow the primary current to build up to its limit of 5.6 A*
(*b*) *Not enough DC bias is present; time t_b is not long enough to allow primary current to build up to 5.6 A*
(*c*) *Too much DC bias is present; time t_c is too long and primary current limit of 5.6 A is maintained for too long a period*

the output from the current sensing comparator are monitored by the dwell period control, which generates a variable voltage according to: (1) the frequency of the signal pulses (the higher the

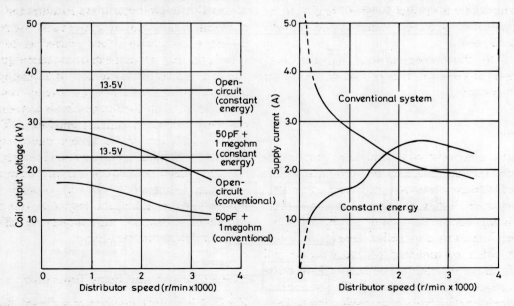

Fig 6.20   *Characteristics of typical 6-cylinder constant energy and conventional electronic systems*

frequency – indicating a higher engine speed – the greater the voltage); (2) whether the comparator output indicates current limiting is occurring (if current limiting does not occur the variable voltage is increased, if current limiting does occur the voltage is decreased). The voltage is added to the signal from the signal generator as a DC bias voltage, which affects the points in time at which the pulse shaper circuit triggers on and off. Fig 6.19 shows how the bias voltage alters the trigger point timing and the resultant effects on the primary current. The combined effects of the feedback loops adjusting the trigger points for engine speed and primary current limit ensure that the situation shown in Fig 6.19(a) is maintained throughout all engine operating conditions. Figs 6.19(a) and (b) show effects on primary current when under- and over-adjusted.

A circuit, the stationary engine cut-off control, monitors the output of the pulse shaper and when no signal is detected (equivalent to the condition where the engine is stopped, but the ignition is on) it switches off the driver stage completely, thus switching off the output stage and no current flows through the primary winding of the coil. Damage to the coil is thus prevented. As soon as the starter motor is operated and the engine turns over, a signal is once more detected and primary current can flow.

Fig 6.20 shows comparisons between performances of constant energy and conventional ignition systems.

Caution

The actual electronic control module contains an integrated circuit, thick film substrate and a high current Darlington transistor mounted on a beryllium substrate. Finely powdered beryllia is toxic and it is inadvisable to open or crush the ECM.

Depending upon application the control module can either be mounted on the wing or coil (away from the distributor) or be attached to the outer surface of the distributor. The mounting must provide satisfactory heat dissipation to keep down the control module's operating temperature.

Performance of an electronic ignition system is extremely high compared with that of a conventional system, to such an extent that contact with live parts or terminals can be fatal. Because of this, the ignition *must always be switched off when performing any work on the system*. If checks on the ignition system or adjustments on the engine have to be carried out with the ignition switched on, extreme care must be taken and test equipment, such as tachometers, timing, lights etc, must be capable of safe operation. Most high tension voltage spikes are absorbed by the capacitance of the vehicle's battery, so reducing danger. Therefore it is wise not to run the engine with the battery disconnected.

Digital electronic ignition systems

The electronic ignition systems discussed so far all use a breakerless distributor complete with centrifugal and vacuum advance devices and therefore do not fully meet the requirements of a modern engine. Digital electronic ignition systems incorporate constant energy and current limiting inductive discharge features too, but unlike the traditional system in which ignition advance is obtained mechanically, a microcomputer is used to calculate the point of ignition and the required timing advance and retard according to engine speed and load. Digital electronic techniques provide a more accurate method of adjusting spark advance timing for the relevant engine conditions, speed, load, temperature, and leads to greater fuel economy and clean exhaust emissions. There is also no variation of the timing due to age and wear of mechanical components. Good starting is ensured, idle-speed control is improved and, most important, detonation (knock) control can be implemented enabling the engine to run close to the knock threshold, thus improving efficiency, without detonation occurring.

System layout and basic functions

Fig 6.21 is a block diagram of a digital electronic ignition system which includes:

1   Crankshaft position sensor
2   Engine speed sensor
3   Engine coolant temperature sensor
4   Engine load sensor
5   Knock sensor
6   Battery voltage sensor
7   Electronic microprocessor-based control unit
8   Ignition coil
9   HT distributor.

Optimum ignition timing for all driving conditions is pre-programmed in the control unit's electronic memory; the actual ignition timing used is determined by the microprocessor, taking into account all input information from the various sensors.

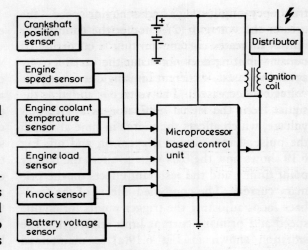

Fig 6.21   *Block diagram of a typical digital electronic system*

Microprocessor signal processing (Fig 6.22)

Information from the analogue sensors measuring manifold pressure, engine temperature and battery voltage is digitised in the control unit analogue-to-digital converter. Engine speed and crankshaft position are already digital qualities and require no conversion. The microprocessor has a quartz crystal oscillator for generating the clock signal, a programmable read only memory (ROM) for permanently stored data, with a random access memory (RAM) for rapidly changing data. Values for the ignition and dwell period are updated in RAM at a rate of 9300 times per minute. These values are recalculated in order to provide the optimum ignition point for the engine

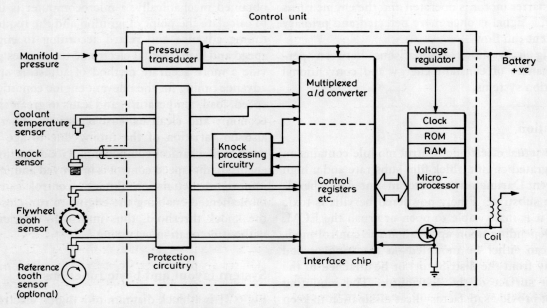

Fig 6.22   *Signal processing within digital ignition control unit*

at any operating speed. The primary circuit of the ignition coil is switched by the power transistor. The dwell period is controlled so that the secondary voltage remains constant irrespective of operating conditions. Fig 6.23 shows, graphically, typical control signals processed by the control unit for the formation of dwell and ignition timing angles.

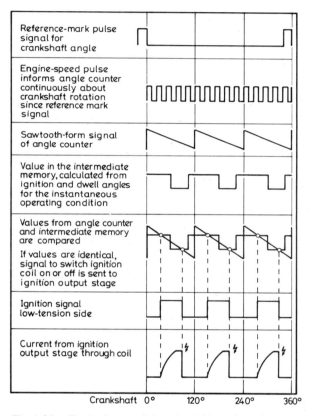

Reference-mark pulse signal for crankshaft angle			
Engine-speed pulse informs angle counter continuously about crankshaft rotation since reference mark signal			
Sawtooth-form signal of angle counter			
Value in the intermediate memory, calculated from ignition and dwell angles for the instantaneous operating condition			
Values from angle counter and intermediate memory are compared			
If values are identical, signal to switch ignition coil on or off is sent to ignition output stage			
Ignition signal low-tension side			
Current from ignition output stage through coil			

Crankshaft 0°   120°   240°   360°

Fig 6.23   Typical control signals within a digital electronic ignition system

Typical systems operation

Stored in the electronic memory of the microprocessor is the basic information on the engine's ignition characteristics. The ignition data is obtained from three dimensional optimum spark advance maps (Fig 6.24) and electronically stored in the form of look-up tables. These memory map

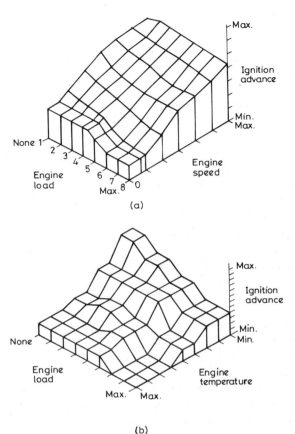

(a)

(b)

Fig 6.24   Typical digital ignition advance characteristics related to engine load and
(a) Speed
(b) Temperature

arrangements give the correct ignition point for each parameter affecting ignition timing.

The actual amount of ignition advancement is determined by adding together the contribution made, by each of the parameters, to the ignition timing. The individual amount of advance for each parameter is contained in the electronic memory's look-up tables. The method of determining the total amount of advance is indicated in Fig 6.25(a) and the associated flow diagram in Fig 6.25(b).

On receipt of a timing pulse from the crankshaft position sensor the microprocessor initiates a count-down counter with the relevant spark timing code (calculated as shown in Fig 6.25) and the

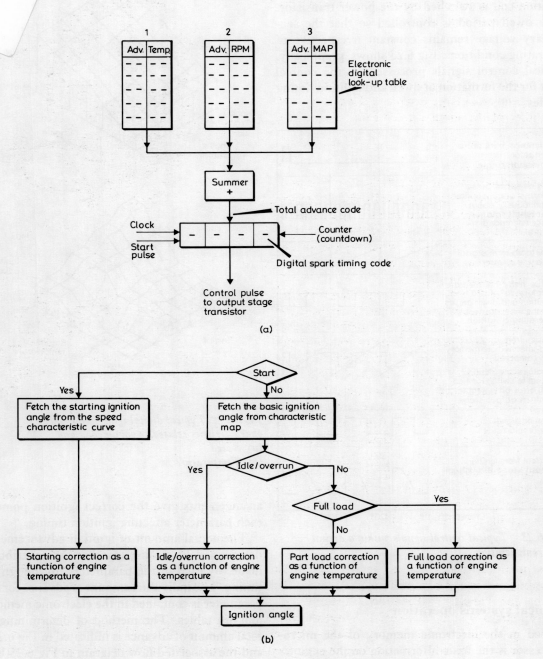

Fig 6.25 *Typical ignition timing advance calculations in a digital electronic ignition system*
(a) *Method*
(b) *Flow diagram*

counter counts down. At zero the output stage transistor is turned off, breaking the primary current and generating a spark.

Sensors

The success of the digital electronic ignition system depends to a large extent on the quality and reliability of the input signals from the various sensors.

Crankshaft sensors

The crankshaft sensor(s) is attached to the crankcase and projects through to the flywheel ring gear or a reluctor disc attached to the engine side of the flywheel face. The sensor armature runs close to the ring gear teeth or between the two sets of reluctor teeth on the reluctor disc maintaining a small but crucial air gap.

When the fly-wheel rotates the air gap varies from a minimum where the tooth is opposite the sensor, to a maximum where the sensor is opposite the gap between the teeth. This varies the reluctance of the magnetic flux path and so generates a voltage at the sensor output terminals. Fig 6.26(a) shows a reluctor disc type of crankshaft sensor assembly. Fig 6.26(b) gives details of the disc itself. As the crankshaft and flywheel rotate the sensor produces a pulse every time a reluctor tooth passes it. The frequency of the pulses is thus an indication of crankshaft speed. At a position representing TDC a reluctor tooth is missing, thus a missing pulse in the received train of pulses indicates TDC to the control unit.

Pressure sensor

The pressure sensor detects the inlet manifold absolute pressure as a measure of the load on the engine and is usually of the semiconductor (silicon bridge strain gauge) pressure-dependent type. This type of sensor allows rapid and fairly accurate load sensing. Possibly, a diaphragm-actuated LDVT pressure sensor or an aneroid diaphragm-operated Hall effect sensor may be used. The pressure sensor is usually mounted within the control unit.

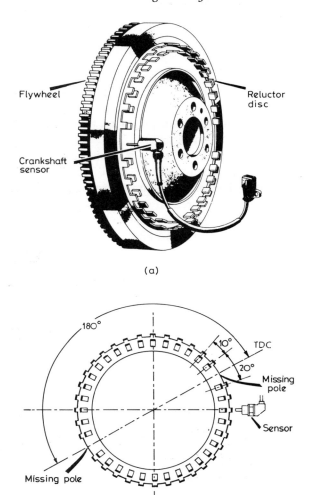

(a)

(b)

Fig 6.26   Crankshaft position and speed detection reluctor disc and sensor
(a) *Assembly*
(b) *Reluctor disc details; The two missing teeth diametrically opposed (180°) correspond to two TDC positions. The other teeth are spaced at 10° intervals*

Engine coolant temperature sensor

Depending on the requirements, either a nickel thin-film temperature sensor or a negative temperature coefficient (NTC) semiconductor temperature sensor is used. The resistance of the sensor material varies with temperature so pro-

viding a measure to be used by the control unit. A typical operative range is −40°C to +140°C.

Knock sensor

The knock sensor is a piezo–electric accelerometer which produces an output voltage proportional to the sensed vibration produced by combustion detonation (engine knock).

Combustion detonation is a condition where the air-fuel mixture in the cylinder does not burn normally. The pressure rise during this burning is so rapid compared to normal combustion that it is accompanied by an audible 'ping' or 'knock'. It is important to avoid knock, though some low level knock may be acceptable for efficient operation. In a mechanical, or conventional electronic, ignition system knock can only be avoided by retarding the engine to the degree where knock never occurs. Under certain operating conditions, however, this means that the engine is retarded by too much a degree and it runs uneconomically, well away from the knock limit (Fig 6.27). A digital electronic ignition system, on the other hand, can be programmed to more closely follow the actual knock limit. Further, a digital electronic ignition system with knock threshold detection i.e. one with a knock sensor, can control and advance the spark timing so that the engine runs, literally, on the knock limit.

The knock sensor and closed-loop feedback system enables the engine to be run with an additional amount of advance right up to the knock limit.

Information from the knock sensor enables the microprocessor to detect when the knock limit has been exceeded on an individual cylinder. At the fourth ignition pulse (or sixth on a six cylinder car) after knock has occurred, timing is retarded in specific steps (3 or 5 degrees) up to a maximum of 20 degrees, until the knocking stops. Once knock has been eliminated ignition point is programmably advanced in steps back towards the memory mapped timing. The actual rate of return to normal ignition in one design is 0.625 degrees/16 sparks.

Electronic control unit

The control unit has two main functions:

1. to control ignition timing, using information received from various sensors, and as required by the ignition map characteristics of the electronic memory

2. to provide a constant energy drive to the ignition coil, controlling the coil primary current as it turns on and off.

A typical control unit consists of an 8-bit miroprocessor-based central processing unit (CPU) containing 2 Kbyte of ROM and 64 bytes of RAM, an 8 bit-timer, a quartz oscillator, multiplexers, and power switching stage.

Analogue input signals from sensors are fed to the control unit where they are converted into digital signals which can be processed by the microprocessor. For example, the signal variables related to pressure, temperature and vehicle voltage are converted first into a proportional time period by means of a charging capacitor. The control unit timer then produces the necessary period-to-digital conversion. Only one variable can be selected at any one time, so they are all applied initially to an analogue multiplexer, the microprocessor choosing which is to be converted.

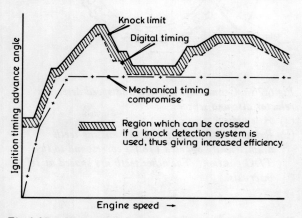

Fig 6.27   Illustrating how digital electronic ignition systems may run the engine close to the knock limit (or even at the knock limit if a knock detection system is used) whereas a mechanical, or conventional electronic, ignition system must run the engine far enough away from the knock limit as to ensure knock does not occur under any conditions

The power stage is controlled by the microprocessor by way of suitable electronic drivers.

Control unit software is designed to process all the real-time events which occur at the same time or in rapid succession up to the maximum engine speed.

Distributorless ignition management

Conventional distributors perform two basic functions:

1   they distribute the secondary electrical energy to the appropriate spark plug in a timed sequence. This is carried out by the camshaft driven rotor, distributor cap and correctly connected HT plug leads

2   they ensure the secondary voltage is created at the appropriate crank angle.

With the introduction of electronics into the ignition system the second function of creating the spark and varying the ignition timing has been removed from most distributors. But the rotor and cap still perform the first function, which is a mechanical function. An alternative to mechanical distribution now exists making the distributor completely redundant, hence the name distributorless electronic ignition.

The electronic distributorless ignition system (Fig 6.28) consists of an electronic control unit, input sensors, and a special ignition coil which combines the functions of coil and distributor. The coil has two primary windings and a double-ended secondary winding. Two ignition amplifiers which switch the primary current in each primary winding, inducing a push-pull effect in the secondary winding spark plugs are selected by the coil (previously a mechanical distributor function) electronically, by the arrangement of high voltage diodes connected to the secondary winding.

When current in the top primary winding (P_1) is switched off a positive voltage is induced at the top end of the secondary winding which fires plug 1, along with a negative voltage at the bottom of the secondary winding which simultaneously fires plug 4.

When the current in P_2 is turned off the opposite polarity voltages are induced in the secondary winding with the positive voltage firing plug 3, and the negative voltage firing plug 2.

The plugs selected to fire together are paired 360 engine degrees apart. This pairing and the

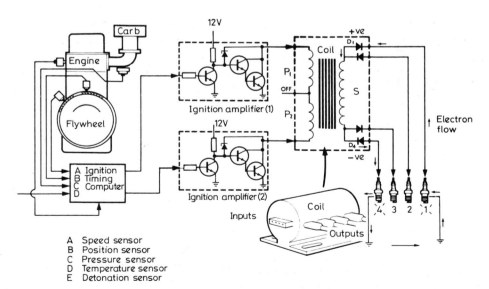

Fig 6.28   Distributorless ignition system. This system, used on the Escort RS 1600i and XR4i, uses a special coil and computer timing control. Computer will probably be shared with fuel management system and amplifiers

timing difference ensures that one of the plugs fires just before TDC on the compression stroke for combustion ignition, and the other fires in a cylinder *on the exhaust stroke*. Firing the plug on the exhaust stroke has no apparent effect on engine performance or exhaust emissions.

In construction, the ignition coil has two primary windings wrapped directly around the secondary, to give the most efficient magnetic coupling (Fig 6.29). The coil must generate a high secondary voltage to fire two plugs at once, the sum of the positive and negative voltages. This does not mean twice the secondary voltage, though, because the plug fired on the exhaust stroke requires a much lower voltage than the plug fired under compression. Also, the plugs do not fire at exactly the same instant, because of the difference in time taken to reach firing voltage. Once the exhaust plug has fired only about 1000 volts is needed to maintain its spark, so the rest of the available secondary voltage can be applied to the plug on the compression stroke, causing it to fire just after the exhaust plug.

Due to the absence of the mechanical distributor all high tension sparks occur within the cylinder, where they are shielded by the engine block thus reducing electromagnet radiation. With plugs firing twice as often as distributor systems, however, plug electrode erosion is increased.

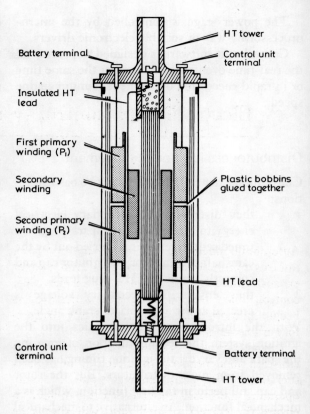

Fig 6.29   Construction of push-pull ignition coil which combines coil and electronic distributor functions

7

Electronic fuel control systems

Automobile engineers are continually striving towards minimal fuel consumption and cleaner exhaust emissions. The application of electronic control, once too complex and expensive, is becoming more and more a remarkably straightforward economical solution.

Engine power, fuel consumption and exhaust emission all depend on the accuracy of the air-fuel ratio. With petrol engines there are many operating conditions under which it is difficult to ensure the correct air-fuel ratio will always be delivered to the engine's cylinders for combustion:

- low operating temperatures, with associated poor vaporisation
- minimum idle speed to support fuel in air stream
- excess fuel for cold starting
- uneven fuel distribution between cylinders
- poor mixing of air and fuel
- acceleration and full load when extra fuel is called for.

When the induced air quantity equals the theoretical air requirements for complete combustion the equivalence ratio (also known as the excess air ratio) is said to be 100% or equals 1. When the induced air is less than theoretical (rich mixture) the ratio is less then 1; 85–95%, or 0.85–0.95. When the induced air is more than theoretical (weak or lean mixture) the ratio is more than 1; 102–120% or 1.02–1.2.

In most cases a narrow band of ratios (0.9 to 1.1) have proved optimal (Fig 7.1). To keep equivalence ratios within these limits the actual quantity of air entering the cylinder must be known so that the precise amount of fuel quantity can be supplied.

Fuel systems, whether carburettor or fuel injec-

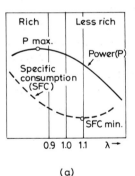
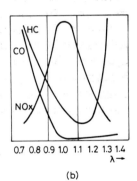

Fig 7.1   Target specification for
(a) Fuel consumption and   (b) Exhaust emission

tion have to deliver the correct air-fuel mixture for each engine operating condition. Over the years the carburettor has been the most common fuel supply system: though it has many disadvantages it is, generally speaking, a cost effective device. Carburettor development and technology has kept pace with the technological developments of the engine to such an extent it is still a very common system.

Electronic carburettors

Digital electronic control techniques are now applied to carburettors to enhance performance. The control system can provide a lower idle speed and overrun (deceleration) fuel cut-off to reduce fuel wastage, as well as electronic control of automatic choke systems. Fig 7.2 shows the benefits of such electronic control procedures in terms of fuel economy:

a) by automatically reducing the time the choke remains in operation fuel consumption can be improved by as much as 5%, compared to a manual choke system.

b) the electronic control allows idle speed to be as much as 100 rev/min below normal rate, giving fuel gains in stop/start driving of 3% overall and 12% on tick-over

c) deceleration fuel cut-off prevents fuel wastage when the engine is not being used to drive the vehicle. The fuel is switched on and off in a 50/50 cycle, half a second off, half a second on, so as to prevent stalling and ensure driveability and smooth operation.

Austin-Rover electronic carburettor

Fig 7.3 shows a typical electronic fuel control system which features an SU carburettor type HIF44 and a Lucas electronic control system.

Stepper motor and choke control action

The electronic choke assembly (Fig 7.4) consists of a housing containing stepper motor, nylon cam, fuel enrichment device and throttle opening pin. The complete assembly is mounted on the side of the carburettor. The stepper motor rotates the fuel enrichment device and the cold running fast idle throttle position by means of the operating pin.

When activated, the stepper motor can rotate up to a maximum of 3 complete revolutions. The cold start enrichment device (Fig 7.5(a)) is a rotary valve which allows extra fuel to be supplied from a passage (A) located in the side of the float chamber to an outlet (F) behind the jet bridge. The device comprises a cylindrical valve body (3 in Fig 7.5(b)) with a single entry hole drilled in its sides and an inner spindle (5) bored out at one end and threaded externally at the other, to which the operations cam gear is fixed. A hole in the side of the spindle goes through to its internal bore and at each side of the hole is a groove which

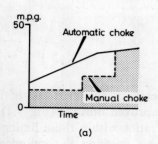

(a)

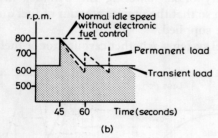

(b)

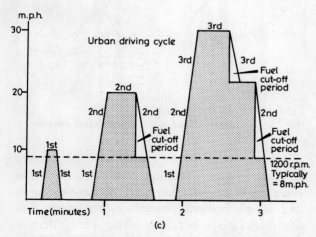

(c)

Fig 7.2   Improvements in fuel economy due to electronic control on carburettors
(a) Choke
(b) Idle speed
(c) Deceleration fuel cut-off

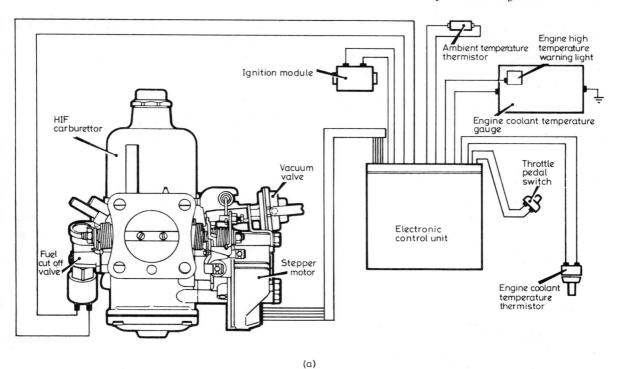

(a)

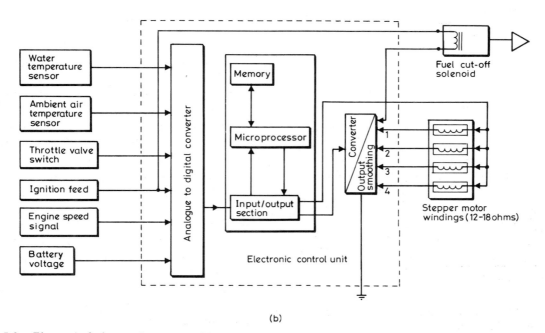

(b)

Fig 7.3   Electronic fuel control system used by Austin–Rover
(*a*) *Main components*
(*b*) *Block diagram*

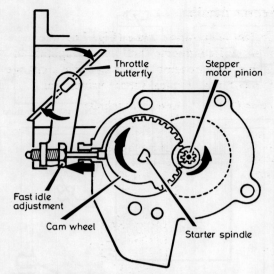

Fig 7.4   Electronic choke actuator mechanism

varies in depth, starting shallow, then deepening as the groove approaches the entry hole. The stepper motor, via the reduction gear, rotates the inner spindle to a position dependent upon sensor data and the engine is turned over for starting. The varying depth of groove as it approaches the entry hole in the spindle ensures that cold start enrichment is progressive.

At the start of rotation of the spindle (1 in Fig 7.5(c)) the shallow part of the groove meets the entry hole in the valve body and, as the motor further rotates the spindle a progressively large passage is exposed until the position is reached where maximum enrichment is provided (2). Fuel flow through the valve is shown in (3).

The complete choke movement is 120° with the first 40° of cam wheel movement providing fast idle and throttle jacking. There are five electrical connections to the stepper motor: one common

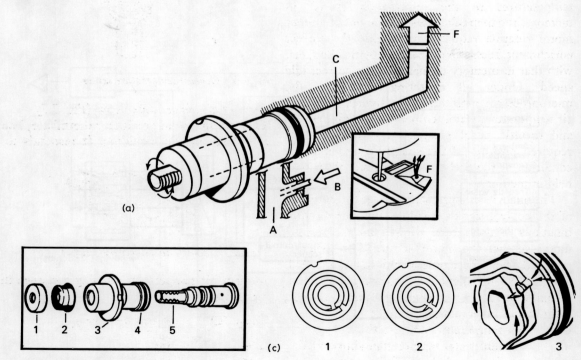

Fig 7.5   Cold start enrichment device
(a) *The complete device*
(b) *Valve assembly*
(c) *Valve orifice arrangement*

live and four returns. The control unit earths combinations of these returns causing the motor to rotate in $7\frac{1}{2}°$ steps giving a total of 150 fuel enrichment and speed combinations.

Electric control unit action

The control unit receives signals from the ignition coil (a measure of engine speed), the air temperature sensor, the coolant water temperature sensor and the throttle pedal switch. The convertor converts any analogue signals into a digital form which can be used by the microprocessor. The input/output section controls the flow of information from the sensors, to the microprocessors and from the microprocessor to the switching stage, and hence controls the action of the stepper motor and fuel cut-off solenoid. The microprocessor compares the air and coolant input temperatures to the information stored in memory, and then calculates the amount of stepper motor rotation required to provide the correct enrichment. It also compares the engine idle speed with that in memory to maintain the correct idle speed. Under all operating conditions the microprocessor monitors input signals regarding air temperature, water temperature, engine speed, and throttle pedal position and calculates the required position of the stepper motor and the condition of the fuel cut-off solenoid, from data held in memory.

The output switching stage, under the influence of the control signals, earths a number of combinations of the return wires from the stepper motor so that the motor is turned to give the required choke enrichment and fast idle speed. The fuel cut-off solenoid is also energised at one-second intervals, for a maximum of nine seconds, if the following conditions are met:

- air temperature above 6°C
- coolant water temperature above 80°C
- engine speed above 1200 rev/min
- throttle pedal in the off position.

Sensor details

Coolant temperature sensor (Fig. 7.6)
The semi conductor thermistor responds to the engine coolant temperature causing a change in its resistance. Typical sensor values are:

Temp (°C)	Resistance (ohms)	
	Min	Max
− 10	8.6 k	− 9.7 k
+ 20	2.35 k	− 2.65 k
+ 40	1.05 k	− 1.25 k
+ 60	550	− 650
+ 80	330	− 360

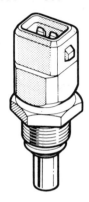

Fig 7.6   Coolant temperature sensor

Ambient air temperature sensor (Fig. 7.7)
This is also a semi-conductor thermistor, housed in a small plastic moulding. It responds to the

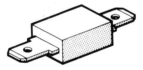

Fig 7.7   Ambient air temperature sensor

ambient air temperature causing a change in its resistance.

Temp (°C)	Resistance (ohms)
− 10	5015
+ 20	1234
+ 25	1000
+ 50	380

Throttle pedal switch (Fig. 7.8)

The throttle pedal switch is mounted on the accelerator pedal linkage, such that the contacts are closed when the pedal is in the idle speed position. The control unit uses the switch to monitor the pedal position when controlling the operation of the fuel cut-off valve.

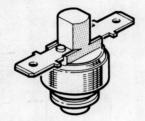

Fig 7.8   Throttle pedal off sensor switch

Actuator details

Stepper motor

A stepper motor is a power device which converts DC pulses into a proportional mechanical movement of its spindle. The speed at which this movement takes place depends upon the rate at which the pulses are applied. The $7\frac{1}{2}°$ step angle of the motor requires 48 pulses to turn one complete revolution. The maximum switching rate at which the loaded motor can start without losing steps is typically 350 steps/sec. The stepper motor used in this application is a 4 phase unipolar type, with a multi-pole stator and permanent magnet rotor. It has stator winding resistances of between 12–18 ohms, a permissible motor temperature of 100°C, a working torque of 4.5 mNm, and a holding torque of 6.5 mNm (approximate values only). It is not advisable to separate the motor from the housing. Repositioning is almost impossible without special equipment.

Fuel cut-off solenoid

Located on the carburettor body, opposite the stepper motor, this valve (Fig. 7.9(a)) opens and closes a passage which links the venturi with the top of the float chamber. When the valve is operated a depression (vacuum) is applied above the

fuel in the float chamber, instead of atmospheric air pressure, preventing fuel supply through the jet to the engine.

Fig. 7.9(b) shows valve operation under normal conditions, with the valve unenergised and closed. Fig. 7.9(c) shows the valve energised and open under deceleration conditions.

Summary of system operation

Fuel enrichment

When ignition is first switched on, with the engine cold, the stepper motor can be heard rotating the fast idle cam to fast idle position and the cold start spindle to maximum fuel enrichment. After starting, as the engine begins to warm up, the motor will step back progressively, reducing the enrichment until the engine is at the normal operating temperature, after which there is no additional throttle opening (fast idle) or fuel enrichment (choke action).

If the engine is started when warm the stepper motor sets the enrichment and fast idle throttle opening to the correct angle depending on the air and coolant temperature at that time. If the air and/or coolant temperature are sufficiently warm on start-up no motor action will be provided for throttle opening or enrichment.

Idle speed control

Consider the engine idling at normal operating temperature as a heavy electrical load is switched on. The alternator will generate more current to meet the load, but this extra resistance to alternator rotation will cause the engine speed to fall below its normal hot idle speed, or even stall. The control unit senses this change in speed and should it be more than 100 rev/min the stepper motor is operated until the idle speed is back at its normal setting, so avoiding the possibility of stalling. The motor is stepped back, gradually removing the throttle opening, to lower the idle speed over a period of some 45 seconds. If the electrical load is still present the throttle will be repeatedly opened and closed until the load is removed.

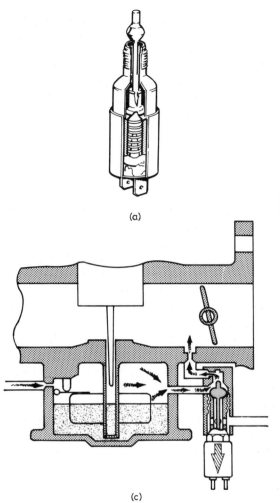

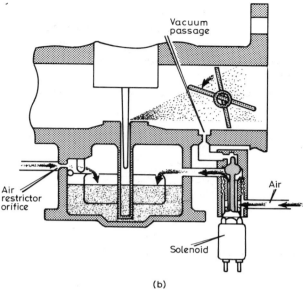

(a)

(b)

(c)

Fig 7.9   *Operation of fuel cut-off solenoid actuator*
(a)   *The fuel cut-off solenoid*
(b)   *Operation during normal running. The solenoid is off and air can enter the float chamber via the solenoid valve and the restrictor orifice. The fuel can be drawn through the jet in the normal way*
(c)   *Operation during deceleration. The solenoid is energised opening the vacuum passage adjoining the float chamber to the venturi. The only air entering the float chamber is through the restrictor orifice, consequently the air pressure above the fuel is reduced and less fuel is drawn through the jet*

Over-run fuel cut-off

The fuel cut-off system operates by opening the solenoid valve which equalises the pressure in the venturi and the float chamber, so that no fuel can be drawn into the engine's cylinders from the float chamber. The system will only operate if certain conditions exist, listed earlier. When these conditions are sensed by the control unit the solenoid valve is opened and closed in one second cycles, causing the fuel to the engine to be shut off, but not for more than one second, so maintaining full driveability.

Bosch–Pierburg electronic carburettor – 2BE

The application of Bosch microelectronics to the Pierburg carburettor gives us a second electronic fuel control system to consider.

Fig. 7.10 shows the system in both layout and block diagram forms. The main components of interest are:

- a choke actuator which is an electromagnetic torque motor
- a throttle butterfly potentiometer
- an electro-pneumatic throttle valve actuator with idle speed switch

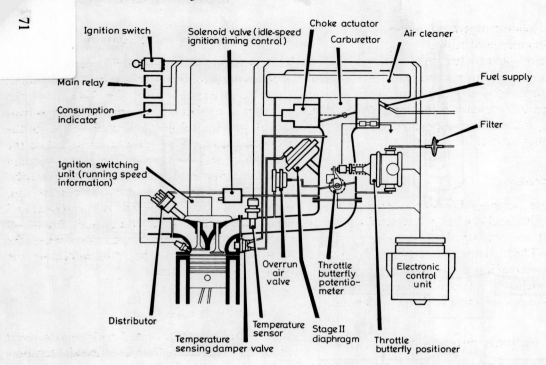

(a)

Ignition switch

Solenoid valve (idle-speed ignition timing control)

Choke actuator

Carburettor

Air cleaner

Main relay

Consumption indicator

Fuel supply

Filter

Ignition switching unit (running speed information)

Electronic control unit

Distributor

Temperature sensing damper valve

Temperature sensor

Overrun air valve

Stage II diaphragm

Throttle butterfly potentiometer

Throttle butterfly positioner

Idle speed sensor

Throttle valve angle sensor

Throttle valve position sensor

Engine speed sensor

Temperature sensor

Signal conditioning and processing interface

Overrun fuel cut-off control

Idle speed control

Starting and warm-up control

Enrichment and acceleration control

Final output stage

Final output stage

Throttle valve actuator

Choke valve actuator

(b)

Fig 7.10   Bosch–Pierburg electronically controlled carburettor system
(a)   Main components
(b)   Block diagram

- coolant temperature sensor
- engine speed sensor
- electronic control unit.

Like the Austin-Rover electronic fuel control system, the Bosch-Pierburg system allows: control of the mixture enrichment during cold starting, warm-up, and acceleration; control of idle speed; overrun fuel cut-off.

Choke actuator

The torque motor used for choke actuation alters the setting of the choke butterfly valve during cold starts and warming-up thus controlling the air-fuel ratio. The high rate of actuation of the control motor also makes it possible to use the choke valve to give enrichment for acceleration purposes. The choke valve can be active in the part-load range.

Throttle butterfly potentiometer

The potentiometer transmits the throttle butterfly setting and any movement of the butterfly to the control unit.

Throttle butterfly valve actuator

This electropneumatic solenoid-operated device operates the throttle butterfly valve to bring about a change in engine speeds. Fig. 7.11 shows the principle of operation. Actuating pressure is controlled by two solenoid-operated valves in the actuator housing. One valve is connected to the atmosphere and the other to the partial vacuum on the inlet manifold side of the throttle butterfly. Both solenoids are activated by the control unit, such that actuator movement is controlled, and hence butterfly position is adjusted. An on/off switch on the actuator plunger closes when the throttle is in idle position, thus informing the control unit of this stroke.

Temperature sensors

The control unit is provided with signals about operating temperature from a semiconductor thermistor, used to measure constant temperature; and a negative temperature coefficient (NTC) thermocouple, used to measure the inside wall temperature of the inlet manifold – a mixed value comprising wall and air-fuel mixture temperatures.

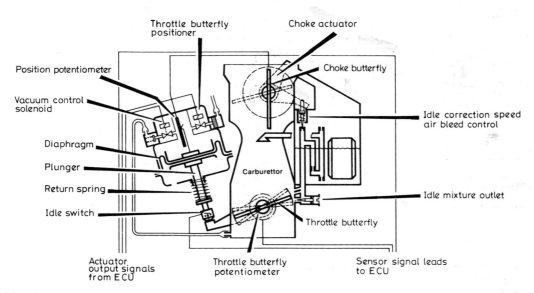

Fig 7.11   Actuator details

control unit

The control unit, a block diagram of which is given in Fig 7.12, uses digital electronic technology. The input section provides an interface to the sensors, generating sensor supply voltages and converting analogue sensor signals into digital signals. The 8-bit microprocessor then calculates the output values as a result of the input variables together with preprogrammed operational curves stored in

System operation

Idle speed control

Idle speed is maintained at a constant value regardless of variation in frictional torque, alternator loading, air temperature, atmospheric pressure and throttle valve wear. The actual idle-speed is continuously measured and compared with pre-determined values stored in memory. If a difference is detected the microprocessor calculates the

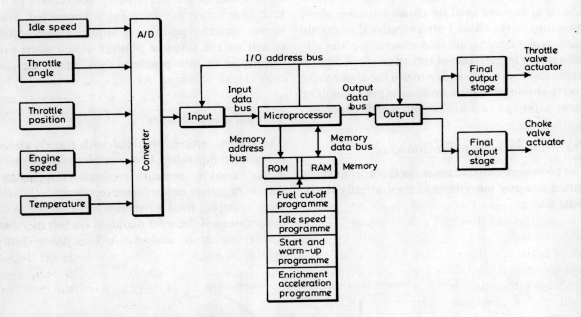

Fig 7.12   *Electronic control unit block diagram and principle of operation*

memory, following a sequence of programmed instructions to obtain the required output values.

The electronic operational curves are stored as data points and linear interpolation is used to represent the curves between the data points. Microprocessor output values are converted into power signals by the output stage and used to control the position of the actuators.

Should the electronic control system fail the carburettor still operates manually because the carburettor is tuned to the desired mixture ratio for stationary operation at normal working temperature. So it is possible to 'limp' home.

new valve angle required, using the deviation between the two speeds, to restore the correct idle speed.

Cold start enrichment

During cold starts, and when the engine is still warming up, fuel enrichment is provided. For cold starts, the choke valve is fully closed and opened progressively as the engine temperature increases. Warm starts have the choke valve angled somewhere between fully open and fully closed, dependent on the measured values of the input signals.

Acceleration

On kick-down of the accelerator pedal, sensed by the throttle potentiometer, the control unit aids acceleration by activating the choke valve to a reduced open position. The closing torque, and length of time, depend on the operating parameters of engine speed, engine temperature, and throttle valve position.

Fuel cut-off

During coasting, over-run, or deceleration the engine is not required to drive the vehicle and therefore needs no fuel. Fuel is cut-off, under the above conditions, when the throttle is below the idle position and the engine speed is above the over-run speed threshold (approximately 1400 rev/min). Under these conditions the throttle valve is fully closed and as the idle mixture outlet is above the butterfly and exposed to atmospheric pressure, there is no pressure difference and the fuel supply from the idle system is cut-off.

The throttle butterfly and choke valves are carefully controlled when the engine speed falls below the lower overrun fuel cut-off threshold, so as to regulate the fuel flow and ensure smooth pickup and driveability as the normal combustion process starts again. To this end, the fuel can be felt to 'cut-in' again if the foot is applied fairly lightly to the accelerator pedal, but if the driver accelerates hard after a period of coasting the fuel supply restarts immediately.

This system is also used to prevent run-on or 'dieseling' when the engine is switched off: the throttle valve immediately moves to the fuel cut-off position, but as soon as the engine ceases to turn the throttle is reset to normal starting position.

Electronic fuel injection systems

Introduction of electronic control to carburettors certainly improves engine fuel consumption and exhaust emissions. Many engine designers, however, believe that such systems still only make the best of a bad deal; and to meet future standards of emission and fuel economy, as well as improving driveability and raise automotive performance, an electronically controlled fuel injection (EFI) system is necessary.

In an EFI system microprocessor-controlled fuel injectors supply the engine with the optimum amount of fuel under all driving conditions. To this end fast acting microprocessors can recalculate an engine's fuel needs 167 times per second.

Major characteristics

With EFI a microprocessor receives electrical signals from various sensors supplying data about air induction volume or mass, engine speed, coolant and air temperature, and throttle position. This information is used to determine the optimum air-fuel mixture for the demands being placed on the engine.

There are three methods of regulating the quantity of fuel injected:

1. continuous injection; where the quantity can be regulated by varying the fuel pressure

2. intermittent injection; where the fuel pressure is constant and the quantity regulated by the time-period during which the injectors are delivering fuel, with phased injection relative to the opening of the inlet valve

3. intermittent injection without timed or phased injection relative to the opening of the inlet valve.

Coupled with these methods, it is possible to have systems using only one injector per engine (single point fuel injection) or one injector per cylinder (multipoint fuel injection). In a comparison (Table 7.1) based on engine performance of all fuel control systems phased (intermittent) multipoint injection seems the obvious choice.

Digital electronic control is preferable to analogue because of speed, reliability, and its cost is on a downward trend. The microprocessor an also be utilised for control of other functions such as ignition, turbo-charging and on-board diagnostics.

Table 7.1 Fuel system performance

	Simple carb.	Electronic carb.	Single point injection	Non-phase multi-point	Phased multi-point
Consumption	□	■	■	■	■
Economy	◪ □	■	■	■	■
Power and torque	■ – ◪	■ ◪	■ ◪	■	■
Emissions	□	■	■	■ ◪	■
Cost	□	■	■	□	□
Reliability	◪ ◪	■	■	■	■
Driveability					
Limp-home	■	■	□	□	□

Key: ■ = Optimum ◪ = Good □ = Normal

Throttle body fuel injection

The phased multipoint injection system has the best prospects for meeting future requirements, and the majority of leading car manufacturers clearly prefer it to any other system. However, in making the transition from carburettors to electronically controlled fuel injection systems, many manufacturers have developed cost effective single-point fuel injection systems, either continuous or unphased intermittently injected, more commonly called throttle body fuel injection systems.

The system combines a single (or twin) fuel injection nozzle, fuel pressure regulator, throttle valve, throttle switch and idle speed regulator into a compact throttle body unit; mounted directly on the inlet manifold, in a similar manner to a conventional carburettor (Fig 7.13(a)). Fuel is injected into the area around the throttle valve, where air velocity is at a maximum; thus ensuring fuel droplets are thoroughly atomised and will be distributed throughout the air mass.

The major controlling parameter for fuel metering is air flow into the engine cylinder, this being measured as air volume by an air flap potentiometer sensor, or as air-mass by a heated wire type sensor. As with other electronically controlled fuel systems, however, several sensing parameters are used to aid cold start mixture enrichment, warm up mixture correction, acceleration, fuel load enrichment, and deceleration fuel cut-off (Fig 7.13(b)).

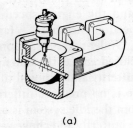

(a)

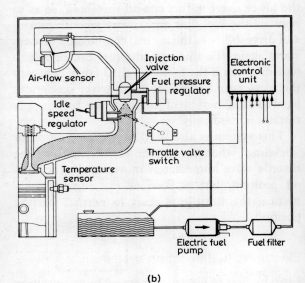

(b)

Fig 7.13 Throttle body fuel injection
(a) Fuel injector valve is mounted over inlet manifold much as a carburettor
(b) Basic electronic throttle body injection system layout

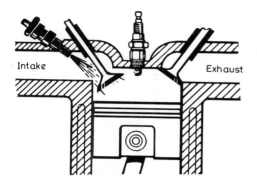

Fig 7.14   *Multipoint fuel injection*

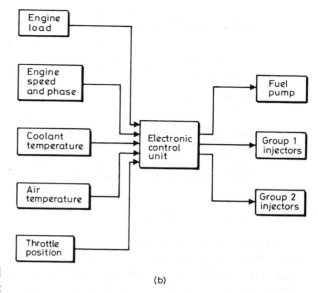

(b)

Intermittent multipoint electronic fuel injection system

In this fuel control system, solenoid operated injectors deliver fuel directly onto the closed, but hot, inlet valve of each cylinder (Fig 7.14). The

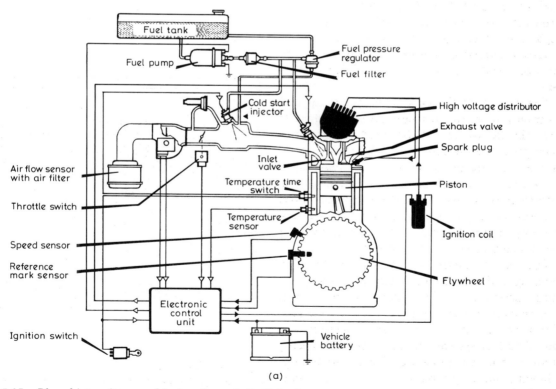

(a)

Fig 7.15   *Phased intermittent multipoint electronic fuel injection system*
(a) *Layout*
(b) *Block diagram*

layout and block diagram of the complete system is shown in Fig 7.15.

The amount of fuel injected is governed by: the volume or mass of air entering through the air-flow sensors; engine speed; throttle position; engine coolant temperatures; and fuel temperature. Sensors measure these variables and pass on the information to the control unit, which computes and controls required fuel flow to suit all engine operating conditions.

Fuel is pumped from the tank through a filter to the fuel distributor pipe from which the individual injectors are fed. Operating pressure is controlled by the fuel pressure regulator.

Cold start enrichment

During cold start a richer mixture is required and so an additional amount of fuel must be provided. Injection of the extra fuel is accomplished: 1) either with a separate cold-start injector, or; 2) by opening the normal fuel injectors for longer periods or more frequently.

Cold start injector method

The cold start injector is a solenoid valve which sprays an additional amount of fuel into a central part of the inlet manifold for a short duration, thus aiding cold starting (Fig 7.16(a)). When off, a spring forces the solenoid's movable armature against a seal. When the solenoid is switched on, the movable armature is forced away from the seal, allowing fuel to flow. The shape of the injector's nozzle causes the fuel spray to swirl and ensures good mixing and suspension of the fuel with the air flow.

To prevent over-enrichment and fuel-wastage, the period for which the cold start injector opens is controlled by a heat sensitive time switch (Fig 7.16(6)), bolted into the engine body. Inside the time switch is a heated bimetallic strip which breaks a pair of electrical contacts after a short period of operation. On a cold start the heat from the electrical winding forces the bimetal strip to open the contacts, breaking the circuit to the cold start injector valve after about 8 seconds at −20°C. With the engine warm, engine heat alone

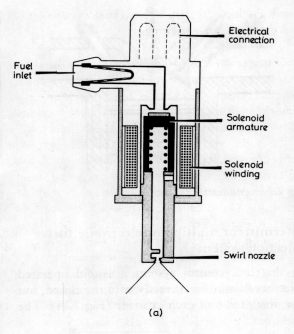

(a)

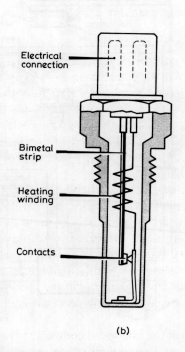

(b)

Fig 7.16   Cold start enrichment by cold start injector
(a) Cold start injector
(b) Heat sensitive time switch

forces the bimetal strip to keep the contacts open and prevent over-enrichment.

Cold start control of fuel injectors

In modern systems the cold start injector is eliminated. Instead, the cylinder injectors themselves meter the additional fuel; though a more complex control procedure is required of the control unit.

When the control unit senses that the engine is being cranked, it provides an open injection period for every ignition pulse, rather than one injection period every second ignition pulse (as for normal running). On cold cranking starts the fuel is injected every 180°; twice per crankshaft revolution on a four cylinder four stroke engine.

Reduction of this large initial fuel quantity takes place after a preset temperature has been reached or a preset number of crankshaft revolutions have been counted by the control unit, after which the fuel quantity is steadily decreased by reducing the length of the injection control pulse. When the engine speed exceeds a preset threshold, say, 250 revs/min, initial cranking enrichment ends.

Idle speed control

The idle speed control device, under warm-up conditions, supplies an extra volume of air in the engine so that it runs at a higher (fast idle) than normal idle speed. The device also regulates the auxiliary air flow to maintain the idle speed within a specified range. It is controlled either by an electrically heated bimetal strip, solenoid or a motor type actuator.

When a load (for example, when headlights are turned on) is applied to the engine when idling, and engine speed drops below the lower limit of the specified idle range, the idle control device opens to increase the amount of intake air and thus increase the idle speed. Similarly, if idle speed increases to exceed the upper limit of the specified idle range the device closes to decrease engine speed.

Main purpose of the idle speed control is to prevent engine stall and engine vibration caused by too low an engine speed. The idle speed, under no load, can be adjusted by the idle adjusting screw.

Acceleration and full load enrichment

During periods of acceleration and full load operation a richer fuel mixture is desirable. The control unit detects acceleration as a rapidly rising signal, and full load as a maximum signal, from the throttle potentiometer. Enrichment is provided by lengthening the fuel injector valve opening times. On deceleration or removal of full load requirements the control unit reduces injector valve opening times.

Electronic control unit

The following description is general but typical of the control units designed to govern fuel injection electronically by processing the input signals from sensors and calculating the correct opening time of the injector valves, so that the required volume of fuel is supplied to the engine.

The input and output circuits of the ECU are routed, via a multipin plug, to the wiring harness which, in turn connects it to the sensors and injectors. Protection circuits are often included against reverse polarity connection and short circuit of the terminals. Signal processing relies on a technique based on error signal composition or a preprogrammed microprocessor technique. There is considerable debate over the advantages of each.

Multivibrator-based control units

As shown in Fig 7.17 the multivibrator based control unit has five functional areas – generally formed by integrated circuits – which form the major portion of the entire circuit.

In addition, roughly 300 discrete components, resistors, capacitors, coils, diodes and transistors are fixed to the pcb assembly. The control electronics can be matched to a wide variety of different engine types by trimming certain resistors.

Signal processing

In the input stage signals from sensors are prepared for processing. Signals from the speed and position sensors are converted into squarewave

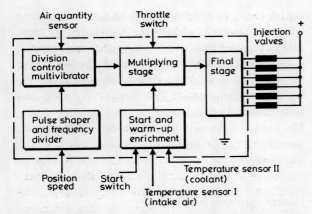

Fig 7.17   Block diagram of a multivibrator based control unit

pulses of the same frequency by the pulse shaper circuit; a monostable multivibrator, processing the signal as shown in Fig. 7.18.

Squarewave pulses from the pulse shaper drive a frequency divider network, located on the same IC chip as the pulse shaper, which divides the squarewave pulses down so that two pulses are created for each complete rotation of the camshaft.

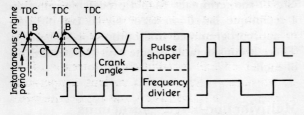

Fig 7.18   Preparation of input signals for further processing. The pulse shaper generates rectangular pulses from the trigger pulses. The frequency divider halves the pulse sequence in order to provide triggering pulses for the injection valves

The frequency divider is based on the bistable multivibrator, which requires one pulse to switch on and another pulse to switch off. The shape of the pulse is still square but of a lower frequency to the shaper pulse. The frequency divider divides the pulse shaper frequency by:

- 2 for a 4 cylinder engine.
- 3 for a 6 cylinder engine.
- 4 for an 8 cylinder engine.

This speed data from the frequency divider is fed along with the air-flow signal from the air quantity sensor to the next stage; the division-control multivibrator. The division control multivibrator converts the air-flow signal into a squarewave control pulse, the duration of which is proportional to the air volume divided by crankshaft speed – so giving the cylinder air charge per induction stroke. This pulse is used to control the fuel injector valves, so the pulse duration correspondingly determines the quantity of fuel which is injected – giving the correct air-fuel ratio for each induction stroke.

Calculation of:

$$\frac{\text{air quantity, } Q}{\text{engine speed, } N}$$

is done electronically by charging and discharging a capacitor in the circuit. The capacitor is charged with a constant current for a time which is inversely proportional to engine speed, then discharged with a current which is inversely proportional to air quantity.

Now, as the charge time is inversely proportional to engine speed the voltage to which the capacitor charges is also inversely proportional to engine speed (i.e. the faster the engine runs, the lower the voltage). The discharge time (t_d), must be directly proportional to charged voltage, so the discharge time is therefore inversely proportional to engine speed.

Further, the discharge time must be inversely proportional to discharge current so if the air quantity is also inversely proportional to discharge time, it follows that the discharge time must be proportional to air quantity.

As the discharge time is both proportional to air quantity and inversely proportional to engine speed, it can be seen that:

$$t_d = K \times Q/N$$

where K is a constant of proportionality and is therefore irrelevant.

Circuit operation can be understood in two examples. First, for a change in engine speed with constant load (Fig 7.19). As engine speed increases from n_1 to n_2 a shorter time is available to charge

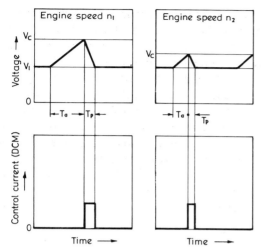

Fig 7.19   Capacitor voltage and pulse duration as a function of engine speed (constant load)

is the same (constant speed) but the discharge current varies, thus changing the discharge time and hence the period for which the fuel injector valve is open. The magnitude of the discharge current (I_d) is linearly dependent upon the air sensor's signal voltage but because $I_d \simeq V_s$, and $V_s \simeq \frac{1}{Q}$, then $I_d \simeq \frac{1}{Q}$.

Therefore it follows that during part-load conditions, when the air volume is relatively low, the signal voltage is high and the capacitor discharge current will also be high. During full-load operations the air volume quantity (Q) is large, the signal voltage is low and the capacitor discharge current is also low; so that it takes longer for the capacitor to discharge. The injection time period is now longer allowing more fuel to be injected to meet the load condition.

the capacity, so the charged voltage is correspondingly lower. The discharge time is dependent on both the charged voltage and the discharge current, but as the discharge voltage is constant (constant load) the discharge time and hence the period for which the fuel injector valve is opened, is dependent on the charged voltage and on the engine speed.

Second, for a change in engine load with constant speed (Fig 7.20). Here, the charged voltage

Multiplying stage

The pulse duration calculated by the division-control multivibrator defines the basic period during which a fuel injection valve is opened in order that the correct air-fuel ratio is maintained whatever the engine load and speed. But the engine requires varying air-fuel ratios when cold starting and decelerating etc, so adjustments must be made to the division-control multivibrator's pulse under such conditions. This is done with the multiplying stage, which collects additional information from the throttle switch, air and coolant temperature sensors, and the start switch, and adjusts the injection pulse duration accordingly.

The multiplier operates on the same principle as the division-control multivibrator i.e. the rapid charge and discharge of a capacitor. The capacitor charge and discharge currents depend on correction signal voltages derived from the signals from the sensors feeding the multiplier. A low coolant temperature, for example, (Fig 7.21) has a significant effect on the discharge current and discharge time and thus the injection duration. Thus when cold starting the injection pulse is much larger than when warmed-up, so much more fuel is injected into the engine. Corrections due to other variables have less effect on the injection time, and in most of these cases the capacitor

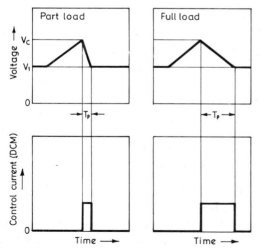

Fig 7.20   Capacitor discharge and pulse duration as a function of load (constant speed)

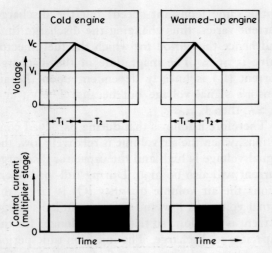

Fig 7.21   *Effects of temperature on the injection pulse duration (multiplying stage)*

charging current is a measure of these less important corrections.

Voltage correction stage

Due to the operating characteristics of the injector solenoid the injection pulse needs further correction to compensate for self-induction, pull-in time, and release time. Without electronic voltage correction these delays would result in an insufficient duration of injection and a weak air fuel mixture.

The pull-in time is very much dependent on battery voltages. Release time on the other hand,

is only slightly dependent on battery voltage. Therefore, the lower the battery voltage the smaller the amount of fuel injected. To compensate for any variance in supply, the battery voltage is fed to the multiplier as a control parameter. The multiplier than extends the injection pulse by an amount equal to the voltage dependent delay of the injector. The extended pulse designed to compensate for voltage change and general delay times is shown in Fig. 7.22.

Final stage

The multiplier can only switch a few milliamps, but currents of 1.5 to 5 A must be switched for each injector. This amplified current is supplied by the final stage of the control unit. The pulses from the multiplier directly trigger the final stage: an integrated circuit Darlington transistor pair (Fig. 7.23).

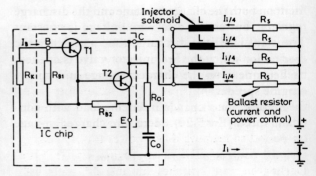

Fig 7.23   *Final stage of control unit*

The pulses from the multiplier are fed to this output IC through a coupling resistor. As soon as base current flows to the base of T_1, both transistors conduct, with the power transistor T_2 connecting the windings of the injectors to the vehicle electrical system's earth for the duration of the injection pulse. All injectors open and close simultaneously.

Injection timing is arranged so that for each rotation of the camshaft, two injection operations take place, each supplying one half of the fuel required by each working cylinder for one air charge.

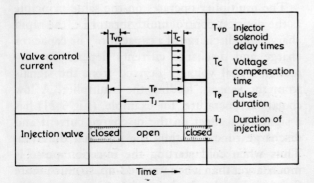

Fig 7.22   *Effects of supply voltage and general fuel injector valve delays on the injection pulse duration (voltage correction stage)*

Current regulation process

The majority of output stages incorporate a current regulator, so that a low holding current can be used to reduce power consumption. At the start of the control pulse from the multiplier the time-dependent injector current increases very rapidly to its maximum value (I_{max} in Fig. 7.24(b)), during which period the injector armature is pulled-in. As soon as the injector armature has completed the pull-in stroke the injector current is reduced to lower holding current for the remainder of the pulse. The holding current (0.5 A) is much less than the pull-in current (2.0 A) but more than the release current (0.25 A).

The current regulator then causes the final stage Darlington pair to switch the injection current on an off in rapid succession. During the on period, the injection current flows through T_2. Should the current increase above the maximum holding current, the current regulator causes the Darlington to switch off. At the same time the current regulator switches a free-wheeling transistor on. The free-wheeling transistor and free-wheeling diode conduct, with the control current decaying back to maximum holding current. This decay current and period is caused by self-induction in the injector windings when the current is switched off. The decay period is longer than the Darlington on-period so keeping down power losses. During a signal control pulse of approximately 6 ms the Darlington pair switches on and off some 200 times.

The current regulator (Fig 7.24(a)) consists of the following functional groups:

- logic circuitry and driver stage
- set point source for maximum load and minimum holding current
- voltage sensor
- comparison circuit
- switching time sensor
- free wheeling stage with free wheeling trigger.

Initially the total injector current produces a time-dependent signal voltage across the measuring resistor (R_M). This signal is fed into the comparison circuit of the regulator. The current

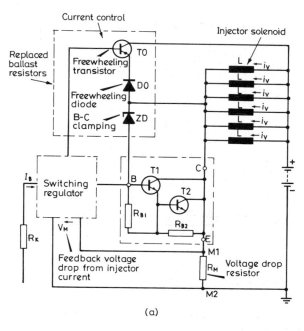

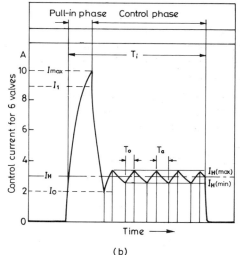

Fig 7.24   Current regulated final stage
(a)   Circuit
(b)   Control current

control phase starts when the pull-in current is almost at its maximum value. This set point is switched from maximum to holding current using the logic circuit and, at the end of the pulse it is returned to maximum current. The voltage sensor (R_M) cannot be used for the lower holding limit because the resistor has no current passing through during the decay period and so no voltage exists across it.

The decay period is set by an RC decay element which sets the Darlington pair's cut-in point during the control phase. During the interval between two control pulses the three transistors are switched off, in an action very similar to the operation of an alternator electronic regulator. The Zener diode keeps the Darlington pair on when the control phase starts. Whenever the self-induction voltage is higher than the breakdown voltage of the Zener diode, the Darlington pair continues to conduct because the Zener diode, when conducting, connects the base of the Darlington pair to the positive supply via the injector windings. As soon as the Zener blocks the regulator drives the Darlington transistors and the current increases for the first time to maximum holding current.

Electronic memory based control units

An alternative to the former method of electronic fuel injection control is that based on a digital control unit using only two LSI integrated cir-cuits: one a ROM pre-programmed with all fuel-ling functions; the other an analogue-to-digital converter.

The ROM stores the fuel schedule as a function of engine speed and load, while the calibration characteristics are smoothed between sites on the memory map by a 32-point interpolation procedure.

The system uses auxiliary wiring boards to provide trimming circuits for acceleration fuel needs, exhaust gas recirculation and feed-back control. The control unit has inbuilt voltage compensation to ensure correct signals are generated. A block diagram and signal processing diagram are shown in Fig 7.25.

Microprocessor-based control units

This type of control unit generates the control pulse for the injector using preprogrammed instructions and electronic characteristic maps stored in memory. Fig 7.26 shows the layout of the control unit which comprises microprocessor, program and data memory, input and output devices, analogue-to-digital converter, voltage

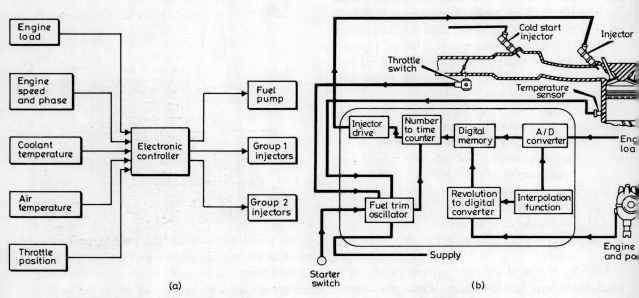

Fig 7.25 *Digital fuel injection control unit*
(a) Block diagram

(b) Signal processing

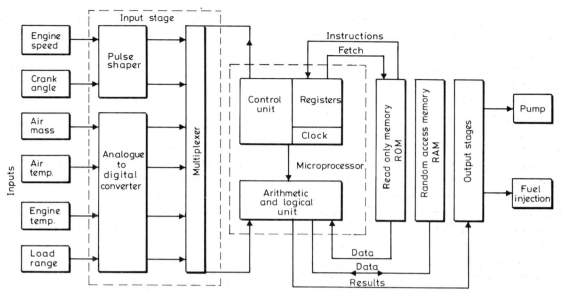

Fig 7.26   Block diagram of a microprocessor-based fuel injection system control unit

source, 6 MHz quartz oscillator; some 200 electronic components. Output power stages are mounted on special cooling brackets for maximum heat dissipation.

The quantity of fuel to be injected per stroke is calculated by the microprocessor on the same basis of input air quantity and engine speed used by multivibrator-based systems. The amount of air taken in on the induction stroke is calculated and used to generate the basic signal for the period of fuel injection. The injector pulse is modified to take into account correction factors to ensure optimum engine operation.

A typical control system may have five or six

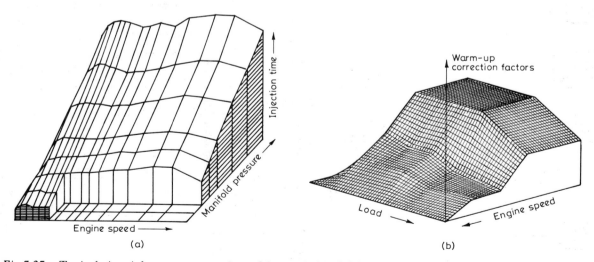

Fig 7.27   Typical pictorial map representations of data stored in ROM regarding
(*a*) *Basic fuel injection valve pulse duration with engine*   (*b*) *Warm-up correction factors to the basic pulse*
      speed and load   *duration with engine speed and load*

sensors measuring various engine operating conditions. These sensor signals are delivered to the input stage of the control unit where the signals are shaped into the required pulses (in the pulse shaper), converted into digital form (in the analogue-to-digital converter), then multiplexed ready for use by the microprocessor.

All instructions for microprocessor operation are stored in ROM along with injection pulse duration data according to engine speed and load (Fig 7.27(a)), and correction data to allow adjustment of the injection pulse duration (Fig 7.27(b)). Operating data from sensors and intermediate calculation results are stored in RAM, updated as required by the microprocessor.

Microprocessor results are converted by the output stage into pulses controlling the fuel pump and fuel injection valves.

System operation
The basic, unmodified injection pulse duration is defined by a number stored in a location of ROM,

addressed by the microprocessor as 8 lines of load and 16 lines of speed data. Engine load and speed are measured by the air mass and engine speed sensors.

Adjustments are made to this basic pulse duration, according to the information received from other sensors regarding temperature, idling, and deceleration. The microprocessor uses this information to address correction data tables and find an adjustment value. Using this value the injection pulse is corrected accordingly.

Fig. 7.28 shows a block diagram of this complete signal processing operation and consequent corrections to the basic injection pulse. A high system clock rate ensures the whole operation is rapid (typically the injection pulse duration can be updated as often as 100 times a second!).

Induction air mass sensor
The precise amount of fuel required by the engine for any given cycle of operation depends initially upon the mass of air inducted during each induc-

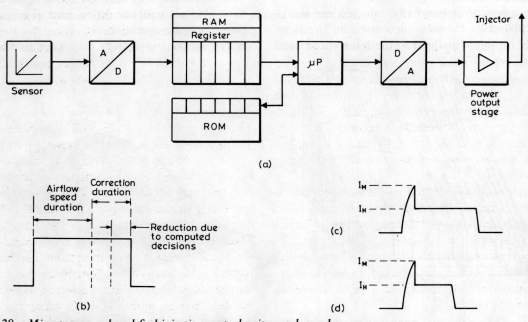

Fig 7.28   *Microprocessor-based fuel injection control unit*
(a) *Signal processing block diagram*
(b) *Basic injection control pulse showing corrections to*

be made
(c) *Basic injection pulse applied to fuel injector valve*
(d) *Adjusted injection pulse applied to fuel injector valve*

tion stroke. The most widely used electronic fuel injection systems operate on two basic parameters: engine speed and air density. These two parameters are used to compute the inducted air mass; because air mass per cycle is proportional to the product of engine speed and cylinder air density. Cylinder air density, in turn, is equal to the product of manifold air density and volumetric efficiency.

Volumetric efficiency for an internal combustion engine can be directly correlated with engine speed, therefore the volumetric efficiency can be computed simply and directly. Cylinder air density, though, cannot be measured directly and has to be determined indirectly from either:

1 absolute manifold pressure
2 air flow quantity and the inducted air temperature.

The air *mass* (rather than air volume) flowing into the engine cylinder must be known because the combustion process is based on the mass of the elements, not their volume. Generally, the massive calculating ability of the microprocessor can derive the air mass more cheaply (using indirect measurements) than measuring the air mass directly.

With the development of the hot-wire air mass flow sensor, air mass can be obtained as a voltage which is converted to a grams per second measurement by the microprocessor. By measuring the mass of air in grams per second, changes in barometric pressure, altitude and humidity are automatically catered for. Then by taking the engine speed into account, volumetric efficiency can be derived.

To take the inducted air measurement the sensor is situated between the air cleaner and the throttle body, so that all the air entering the engine passes through the air sensor. The construction and operation of the three types of sensors used to provide a primary input signal to the electronic fuel injection control unit have been covered in the chapter on sensors.

Throttle body

The throttle body is not only used to hold sensors

for input data to the control unit, but also to hold actuators for some of the output functions. The three main devices on the throttle body are:

1 the throttle butterfly valve – connected to the accelerator pedal so that the air flow rate and hence engine speed can be controlled. Stops are also provided to limit the maximum throttle opening and to initially set the idle speed.

2 a mixture adjustment control – an air bypass, whose air quantity does not pass through the air sensor and therefore cannot affect the fuel delivery, but which enables minor adjustments to be made to air-fuel mixture and CO-content.

3 the throttle position sensor – microswitches or a potentiometer are used to sense the throttle butterfly position; and ensure certain conditions are fulfilled before the control unit makes a decision. The switches and potentiometer provide information as to when the throttle butterfly is in the idling (minimum) or full load (maximum) position. The potentiometer allows the control unit to detect acceleration or deceleration, by a rapidly varying signal. It is important that the throttle body switches are correctly set to ensure efficient operation.

Fuel pump

The fuel pump is a roller-cell type driven by a permanent magnet electric motor. Pump and motor are combined in a common housing surrounded by fuel which cools the electric motor and preheats the fuel. Fig 7.29 shows that the roller-cell pump comprises a housing in which there is an eccentric rotor. On the rotor's outer edges are pockets which house the rollers. When the electric motor is switched on the rotor is rotated at high speed and centrifugal force acting on the rollers force them outwards, where they can function as rolling seals. A pumping action occurs as the eccentric rotor and the roller seals, periodically form an enlarging volume (which creates a partial vacuum) at the inlet and a decreasing

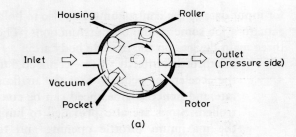

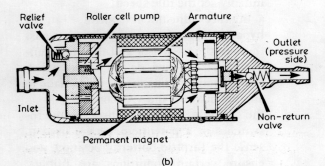

Fig 7.29 *Construction of electrical fuel pump*
(a) *Roller-cell pump*
(b) *Cross-section*

volume (creating a higher pressure) at the outlet.

Fuel from the pump outlet flows over the armature and brush gear, ensuring that the motor housing is full of fuel, and out via a non-return valve. There is no risk of combustion or an explosion occurring because there is never any oxygen present to form an ignitable mixture. Even when the fuel tank is empty of fuel there is still no risk of fire, for the rollers maintain their seal due to centrifugal force – trapping the fuel in the motor housing.

The pump delivers more fuel than is required by the engine so there is sufficient pressure in the fuel system at all normal operating times. A pressure relief valve protects the system from too high a fuel pressure releasing excess fuel back into the fuel inlet side. A non-return valve prevents fuel draining back when the ignition is switched off. A safety circuit is usually included which switches the pump off when the ignition is on but the engine is stationary, as for example after an accident, or simply running out of fuel. When

initially switched on the pump will operate for a short period in order to build up the pressure in the fuel lines. It will not operate again until a cranking signal indicates the engine is turning. The electrical supply from the pump relay may contain a 1 ohm ballast resistor, which can be bypassed on cranking to ensure a sufficiently high supply voltage is maintained.

Interia switch
An inertia switch is incorporated in the fuel pump's electrical circuit which breaks the circuit if, say, the vehicle is involved in a collision. Under such a condition the mass inside the switch is subject to inertia forces due to the sudden change in vehicle speed and moves against a spring loaded switch to open internal contacts.

Fuel filter
A filter (Fig 7.30) is fitted between the pump and the fuel rail so that impurities are filtered out of the fuel. The paper element of the filter should be changed every 48 months or 48,000 miles (80,000 km) or more frequently if subject to abnormal fuel impurities.

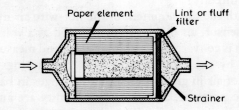

Fig 7.30 *Fuel filter*

Fuel pressure regulator
The fuel pump works in conjunction with the fuel pressure regulator to maintain a fuel supply pressure to the injector valves of about 250 kPa, referenced to the inlet manifold pressure, rather than atmospheric.

Fig 7.31 shows the operating principle and construction of the pressure regulator. Fuel pressure causes the diaphragm to move up, against the pressure spring. At a high fuel pressure the valve opens and allows fuel to return to the tank, so

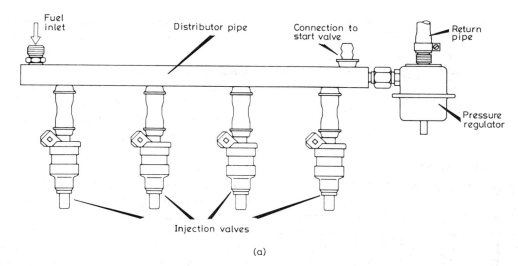

(a)

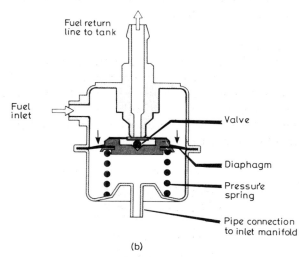

(b)

Fig 7.31 Operating principle and construction of fuel pressure regulator
(*a*) *System configuration*
(*b*) *Cross-section*

lowering the fuel pressure. A connection to the inlet manifold adjusts the fuel pressure regulator so that fuel pressure is with reference to inlet manifold pressure.

Caution

The pressure in the fuel lines must be relieved before removing or disconnecting components for renewal or testing. This will prevent the highly volatile petrol from being sprayed out and thus avoid fire risk.

The fuel pipes may be depressurised by preventing the fuel pump from operating then cranking the engine over for several seconds. The engine may fire until the pressure is reduced.

Injectors
The fuel injectors are solenoid poppet-valves (Fig 7.32) designed to deliver fuel to each cylinder, indirectly, at a pressure of 250 kPa. In some injectors a pintle tip is used to enable the fuel to be atomised efficiently. Generally a needle valve is held on its seat by a small coil spring and is integral with the injector armature. The solenoid winding is mounted in the centre section, with the con-

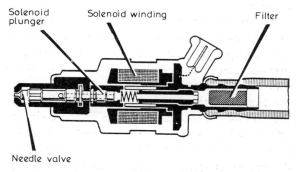

Fig 7.32 Fuel injector solenoid valve

nectors mounted in the rear section. When the injector current is switched on the needle valve is raised some 0.1 mm–0.15 mm from its seat, for approximately 1.5 to 9.0 ms – the actual amount of time the injector stays open depends on the injection pulse duration from the control unit. The opening and closing lag time for the injector is a constant 1–1.5 ms.

Nominal fuel flow at 20°C and 250 kPa supply pressure is 185–200 ml per minute under static test conditions, and 6–8 ml per 1000 injections at 2.5 ms pulse width and 100 Hz pulse frequency.

Some new injectors use a small disc armature to provide the lowest practicable moving mass and thus have rapid opening and closing times. The design of the injector eliminates the need for the injector pintle, giving a nominal fuel flow at 20°C and 250 kPa supply pressure of 388 ml per minute under static conditions, and 11.8 ml per 1000

injections at 2.5 ms pulse width and 100 Hz pulse frequency.

Fuel injector valve control

In the traditional types of electronic fuel injection systems, such as those already discussed, fuel is injected simultaneously from all four injector valves – or in six and eight cylinder engines, in banks of three or four injector valves. In more advanced systems, on the other hand, fuel is injected from one injector valve at a time; just prior to the opening of the inlet valves of the corresponding cylinders.

Such phased injection, sometimes known as sequential injection, provides the optimum fuel required in each cylinder – directly to the cylinder, just outside the inlet valve, at the place where the fuel can best mix with the inducted air. However, phased injection alone cannot adequately cope

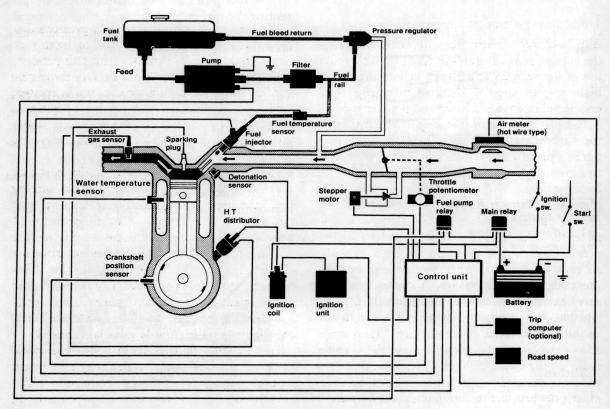

Fig 7.33   Typical combined microprocessor-based ignition and fuel injection system

with the fuel enrichment requirements of the engine. Accordingly, phased injection systems generally switch to a simultaneous injection mode when fuel enrichment is required.

Microprocessor-based combined ignition and fuel injection systems

A great number of components in microprocessor-based ignition and fuel injection systems are used in both systems, and there is little reason why the two cannot be integrated into a single system performing both tasks yet using much fewer than twice the number of components – such is the advantage of microprocessor control. Increasingly, vehicles are being produced with integrated ignition and fuel injection systems (Fig 7.33), but the principles are no different to those discussed in these last two chapters; the single microprocessor merely controls both operations.

Turbocharger electronic control

A turbocharger compresses and pumps inlet air to the engine, providing an increase in the air pressure of between 25 and 50 kPa at intermediate to high engine speeds, thereby increasing both engine volumetric efficiency and performance.

Exhaust gases from the engine are ducted to the turbocharger unit (Fig 7.34) and drive an internal turbine wheel, which is directly connected to a compressor (an impeller) through which the inlet air flows. The boosted inlet air pressure is therefore related to the rate of exhaust gas flow driving the turbine/compressor arrangement. The faster the exhaust gas flow, the higher the inlet air pressure. It is not desirable to have excessive air pressures, because they lead to high cylinder pressures and excessive rises in combustion pressure causing detonation and mechanical damage. The boosted air pressure is, instead, controlled by an exhaust wastegate valve which, when open, allows the exhaust gases to bypass the turbine, reducing the speed of the compressor and thereby reducing the air pressure. In a practical arrangement, air pressure is limited to approximately 50 kPa.

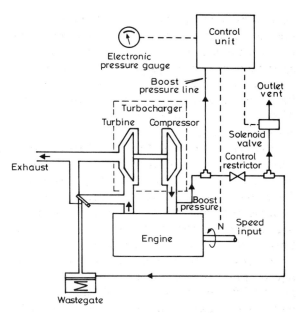

Fig 7.34   *Turbocharger electronic control system*

The wastegate is controlled by a pressure diaphragm actuator which is connected to the air pipe so that the wastegate opens when inlet air pressure is greater than spring pressure. To vary the engine speed at which maximum air pressure is created, a solenoid pressure reducing valve operates to release air and thus lower the pressure, under supervision of the control unit which constantly monitors air pressure.

Sometimes, a wastegate valve in the inlet side of the turbocharger is used to prevent surging when the throttle is closed suddenly at high speeds, causing a rapid rise in air pressure. A throttle sensor detects the closing throttle and the control unit opens the inlet wastegate, directing air from the air pipe back to the turbine. This dampens the rapid pressure rise which could otherwise cause the engine to surge. The control unit then ensures that the inlet wastegate closes smoothly when the throttle valve is reopened.

To maximise the benefits of boosted air pressure over a wider engine range may also retard ignition timing to prevent detonation. The amount of ignition retard can be directly in relation to the air pressure and engine speed; or controlled by means of a feedback loop employing a knock sensor.

Electronic control unit

The control unit is designed to modulate turbo-charged boosted air pressure as a function of engine speed. It incorporates a pressure sensing transducer, circuits to monitor engine speed, an output stage to drive the solenoid actuator valves and adjust ignition timing, speed limiter and indicator circuits. The actual engine requirement is determined from engine speed and compressor boost pressure as measured by the boost pressure sensor.

Digital or analogue circuit techniques are used in the control unit to compare monitored signal levels to those required. The error signal between the sensed pressure and pressure required is processed to generate a square wave of single frequency but with a variable markspace ratio, used to operate the solenoid valve in the wastegate connection. The solenoid valve thus operates at a constant frequency and by varying the square-wave's markspace ratio the valve's open and close time is altered and the pressure to operate the wastegate actuator and therefore the boosted air pressure can be varied to suit engine requirements.

Safety circuits

If the wastegate fails to operate and so the boosted pressure becomes too high the fuel pump relay is switched off or the ignition is interrupted – thus limiting the engine speed and maintaining a safe working pressure. Sometimes, a pressure sensitive safety valve is used instead, venting the excess pressure to the atmosphere.

Similarly, overspeed of the engine is prevented by opening the wastegate at a predetermined engine speed, or by cutting the fuel or ignition at a predetermined speed.

An electronic display is generally provided which lights up progressively as the boost pressure in the turbocharger system increases above normal atmosphere. One manufacturer's system uses 10 LEDs which progressively light up so that when maximum allowable pressure is reached all of the LEDs are on.

Electronic control of engine valve timing

Variable valve timing gives improved cylinder filling (volumetric efficiency) and hence better performance at high engine speeds. Low speed performance can be improved, too, by variation of valve timing in order to reduce mechanical losses. There are accompanying improvements in fuel economy and reduced exhaust emissions.

Valve timing control can only be undertaken effectively on twin-cam engines, as inlet and exhaust valves require different adjustments. Two systems are common. In the first, control is applied, only to the inlet valves, via a hydro-mechanical system with microelectronic control; giving wide angular rotation for greater valve overlap at high speeds, and a delayed action at light load throttle openings for economy. The movement of inlet camshaft relative to the crankshaft is effected by the hydraulic mechanism incorporated within the timing chain sprocket on the drive end of the camshaft (Fig. 7.35). This drive coupling is operated by engine oil pressure, with radial displacement of the camshaft in relation to the gear being actuated by an internal angular piston, giving a timing advance of 10 to 16 degrees.

Oil is fed to the piston through a gallery in the camshaft, with the flow regulated by a central spool valve, operated by an external solenoid actuator. An external spline on the piston couples it to the meshing outer sleeve carrying the camshaft gear, while its annular bore engages a helical gear on the camshaft. When the engine speed increases to a threshold of 1600 rev/min the solenoid plunger opens the valve, and oil pressure is applied to the piston moving it inward. This axial movement of the piston rotates the helical gear, which turns the camshaft in relation to the drive chain wheel.

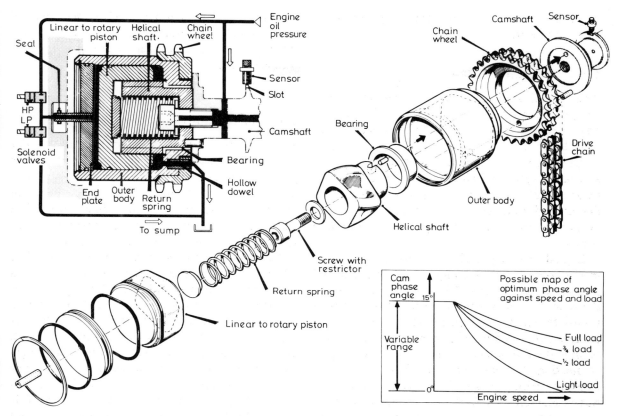

Fig 7.35   Cross-section and exploded diagram of a variable valve timing mechanism

Electronic control

The measured variables used for deciding the control angle are inlet manifold pressure (i.e. engine load), crankshaft speed, and throttle position.

Valve timing control angles are determined by the microprocessor from the desired power (throttle position) and measured engine speed, using digitised maps of engine data based on 256 critical reference points.

The control system holds the normal valve timing for as long as possible, prevents any jerk when changing angles, and makes the adjustments in less than one second.

In the second variable valve timing system the inlet and exhaust camshafts are both controlled

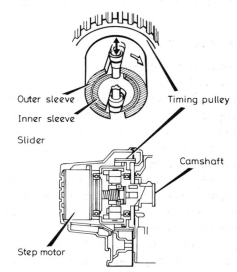

Fig 7.36   Stepper motor controlled variable valve timing cam shafts

(using separate mechanisms) to create optimum inlet and exhaust valve timing and overlap. The electronic control signal is used to actuate a stepper motor (Fig 7.36), which moves a slider in the inner sleeve along a groove in the outer sleeve. The groove is at an angle, so the inner sleeve rotates up to 10 degrees within the outer sleeve as the slider moves.

8

Vehicle control electronics

An engine will operate most efficiently when the gear ratio is such that fuel consumption is minimised while the engine power is sufficient to maintain the required road speed. Transmission electronic control units are designed to optimise the selection of a gear ratio, either in continuously variable or stepped transmission units. They can also be used to engage higher gear ratios (overdrive) during cruising to bring about considerable fuel savings. Widespread gear ratios give the best possible fuel economy, and a 5-speed gearbox leaves much smaller variants between its performance curve than, say, a 3-speed gearbox.

The electronic control is usually based on a single chip microprocessor and separate memories. Input information comes from a variety of operational sources including engine speed, road speed, throttle angle and a digital code for gear selection. Output circuits are used to drive stepper motors or solenoids to control various actuators including clutches, hydraulic pressure lines and oil pump feeds.

The actual transmission control is achieved through a system of memory mapped parameters including gear ratio, rate of ratio change and hydraulic line pressure. Clutch control is based on the functions of throttle angle and engine speed, stored in memory and summed to bring an output signal to the actuator. Usually an automatic transmission system down-rates the vehicle performance figures. But, with electronic control (in comparison with a manual system) only the maximum road speed suffers, down by about 5 to 10 mph. There is negligible effect on acceleration characteristics.

Beside providing precise transmission control responding to both driving and engine conditions, the control unit can be programmed to adjust the gear change points and clutch lock-up operation to provide the driver with a choice of three different driving modes:

1   normal – for almost all urban driving conditions and motorway driving

2   economy – allows more fuel-efficient driving by increasing the operational range of the lock-up clutch

3   power – provides the engine's full power characteristics, so that the driver can have a little extra acceleration for, say, overtaking, or power when pulling heavy loads.

Many advanced transmission control systems are equipped with a self-diagnostic capability to detect malfunctions in the sensors, electrical system and in other areas.

Electronically controlled automated manual gearbox

The main advantage of a direct-drive manual gearbox is its fuel efficiency when compared to hydraulic torque converters and automatic transmission systems. The application of electronic control to a manual gearbox, however, combines

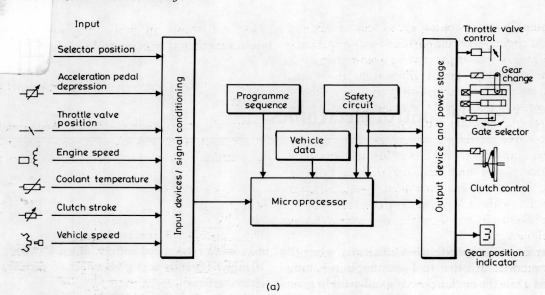

(a)

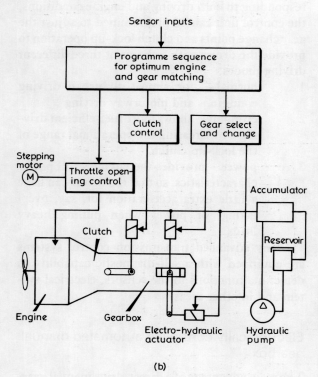

(b)

Fig 8.1   Electronically controlled automated manual gearbox
(a) Block diagram
(b) Operation

the benefits and virtues of manual transmission and the 'easy-to-drive' fully automatic transmission.

The basic transmission is usually a straightforward two-shaft, fully synchronised five-speed gearbox. The clutch is a conventional single dry-plate type with a diaphragm spring. Both clutch operation and gear changing are done by hydraulic actuators, one actuator for the clutch, one for the gear gate selection and a third for the actual gear changing, each of which is actuated by a solenoid valve controlled by an 8-bit microprocessor. An electronic pump provides hydraulic pressure and an accumulator stores and controls the oil pressure. The control unit also controls the opening of the throttle valve by means of a stepping motor, and directs the actuators and stepping motor to do all the clutch engagement and disengagement, gear changing and throttle synchronisation. Sensors provide the input signals related to: engine speed; gear lever position; accelerator pedal depression travel; throttle valve opening; coolant temperature; gearbox input shaft speed; vehicle speed; and the amount of clutch stroke in current use. The control unit controls the the clutch and gear operations by programmed instruments, and performance and specification maps, choosing the optimum clutch operating speed and timing and the best engine/gear combination for the operating condition, as well as preventing over-revving.

The control programs allow fully automated and manual gear changes. Safety circuits are built-in to prevent accidentally moving the gear lever into reverse position while travelling at speed, and to cover the failure of sensors. The software program provides a 'kickdown' function based on a vehicle speed map and the throttle position sensor indicating full throttle. Dependent upon the speed of throttle movement the ratio will be changed down by one (light throttle) or two (heavy throttle) gears.

The interface between the driver and the control system is by either a console selector lever moving through the familiar H-plus-a-leg gate or by push-button selection. Both provide manual and fully automated gear changes. There are four forward gear positions: 1 and 2 – which hold first and second gears respectively; 3 – an automatic mode in which the gears change from 1 to 2 and down through the same gears; D – fully automatic using all five forward gears; and R – reverse hold. The final selection is N – neutral.

Fig 8.1 shows in block diagram form the microcomputer system control and functions.

Automatic transmission electronic control system

Current electronic control units whether intended for constant velocity (CV) or stepped automatic transmissions, have much in common with the

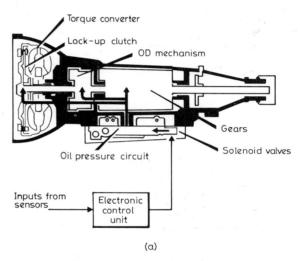

(a)

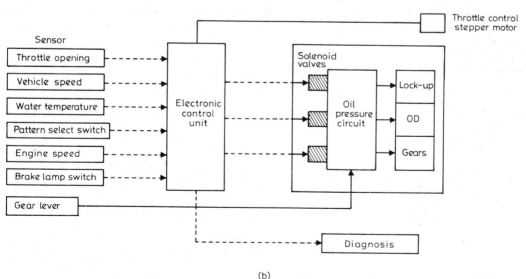

(b)

Fig 8.2   Electronic transmission control system
(a)   Construction of gearbox
(b)   Block diagram

tems already encountered. Where
microprocessor-based and the main
lude sensors for: engine speed; engine
load; road speed; intermediate speed; throttle
angle; brake input; and a digital code sensor for
indicating gear selection, as well as output circuits
suitable for driving stepper motors or solenoids to
control; clutch; gear ratio; hydraulic pressure
lines; oil pump feed; and engine braking (Fig
8.2(b)).

The electronic controlled transmission system
(Fig 8.2(a)) comprises a torque converter with a
lock-up clutch, epicyclic gearbox and a control
unit which calculates optimum points for gear
change and lock-up action, and controls gear
changes, overdrive selection and clutch lock-up
with corresponding solenoid valves.

Control action

Transmission control is achieved through a system
of memory mapped parameters such as gear-
change characterisation, rate of ratio change and
hydraulic line pressure. Fig 8.3 shows a typical
gear ratio change schedule for all operating
conditions, stored as a digital code mask – programmed into the ROM during manufacture. The
point of gear-change is defined by the parameters
which are addressed by lines of load and speed.
Clutch control is based on functions of throttle
angle and engine speed. Both functions are stored
in the memory and are summed to give an output
signal: this time proportional to the clutch pressure required.

A kick-down facility gives a lower gear ratio for
high acceleration needs. The kick-down control
also prevents the kick-down function from taking
place while driving in overdrive gear at speeds
over 100 km/h, to prevent the engine from over-
revving.

Overdrive (OD), is selected with a control
switch and an indicator lamp informs the driver
of overdrive operations. The control unit only
allows OD to be selected, however, under certain
driving conditions. A solenoid controls OD
engagement.

Sensor input signals are conditioned in the peripheral unit (Fig 8.4) to limit voltage amplitudes,
filter out noise and convert the analogue input
signals into digital form. By processing the input

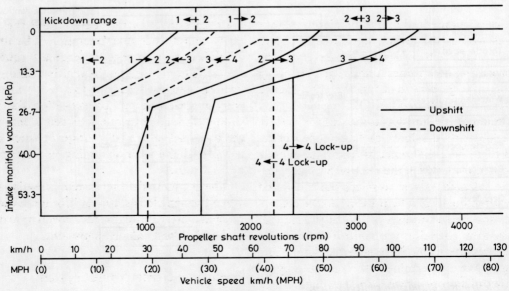

Fig 8.3 *Gear change schedule including kickdown and torque converter lock-up. The full-load gear change points
are reached at higher speeds than in the economy programme*

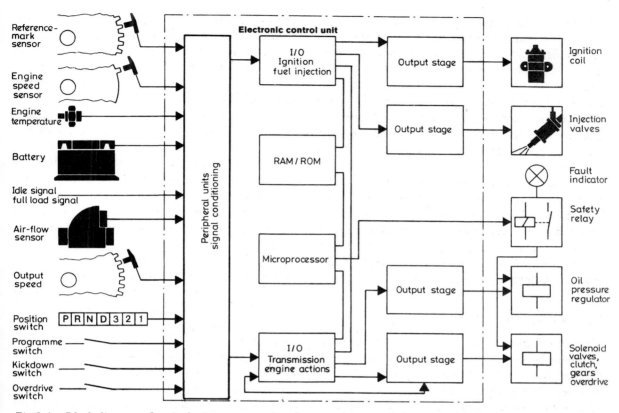

Fig 8.4   Block diagram of typical microprocessor-based automatic transmission system

quantities of engine load and transmission output speed, as well as the switch signals of full-load, kickdown, OD and programme selection, the microprocessor determines a speed for changing down or up a gear ratio using the gear change characteristic map stored in ROM.

The microprocessor then compares the vehicle speed code with the look-up table speed code. Should there be a difference an error speed code is computed from which the microprocessor energises the solenoid valves; to select the calculated gear by directing hydraulic pressure to the control clutches and brake band servo. To ensure smooth and easy gear changing the control unit modulates oil pressure using a pressure regulator. The microprocessor determines the most appropriate modulation pressure using the engine load signal and stored characteristic map.

Many electronic transmission control units gen-erate an output to the ignition and fuel control units, to influence their operation. The advantage of such outputs is that the engine torque can be controlled by retarding the ignition timing during gear changing (to cut out the 'jerk') to ensure a smooth gear change. By retarding the ignition timing the engine torque achieved is only equal to the part-load value. After the gear change has been completed the ignition timing is returned to its normal value.

The output to the fuel system is used to indicate when the vehicle is stationary for more than a few seconds; interrupting the fuel injection to conserve fuel and reduce exhaust emissions.

Electronic cruise control system

A system which allows the driver to select and automatically maintain or resume a constant speed, independent of road conditions, is popularly called cruise control.

The driver initially sets up the electronic control unit to store the vehicle speed at that moment and start the automatic control procedure. The selected speed is stored in memory and compared continuously with later vehicle speeds. Any variation between the two speed signals causes the control unit to adjust the throttle to counteract the difference so maintaining the required vehicle speed. It is also possible to resume to the stored speed after, say, braking or acceleration.

The cruise control cuts out automatically when the brake or clutch pedal is depressed, thus enabling engine braking on overrun and preventing excessive revving on gear changes. Also, to ensure a progressive and steady change in speed and to be responsive to changing road conditions in a way that is comfortable to driver and passengers the system restricts the rate of acceleration to an acceptable level.

Most cruise systems employ an electro-pneumatic system for the mechanical operation of the throttle. Fig 8.5 shows a block diagram of a typical system. Input signals are taken from a magnetic speed sensor (positioned in the transmission line or speedometer cable), the throttle position switch and potentiometer, and the driver select switch. The control unit compares the stored speed with the actual speed and produces a throttle control signal relative to the difference between the two which is applied to the throttle actuator. The throttle actuator sets the engine throttle butterfly valve position to cause the vehicle to speed up or slow down to the desired speed. The actuator control signal is the sum of the control voltage and the signal position of the throttle.

Principle of operation

The majority of control units are of a digital nature, generally microprocessor-based, although analogue systems do exist.

When digital techniques are used the stored speed and the actual vehicle speed are processed directly as binary digital numbers. The speed sensor's input signal is in the form of a pulsed AC voltage whose frequency is proportional to vehicle speed. After amplification and conversion to a square wave, the signal is counted by a binary

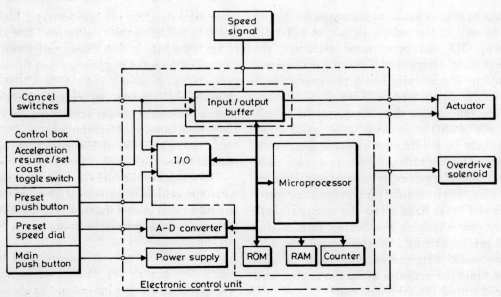

Fig 8.5   Typical microprocessor-based cruise control

counter over a given time period. The number of pulses counted during the period is directly proportional to the vehicle's speed.

The two digital numbers, stored speed and actual vehicle speed, are then compared and (by subtraction) the difference is obtained. The difference is used to generate a control signal for the actuator.

Fig 8.6 shows a cross-section of a typical electro-pneumatic actuator. When the solenoid is energised the armature is attracted to the core,

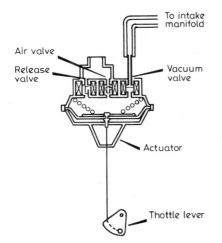

Fig 8.6   Solenoid-operated throttle actuator

closing the air valve and opening the vacuum valve. Vacuum from the inlet manifold draws the diaphragm into the actuator chamber, producing the force for throttle actuation. The force exerted by the piston can be varied by rapidly opening and closing the valves, thus changing the average pressure in the chamber.

The actuator is mounted on the engine and connected directly to the throttle. The control function remains stable in all driving conditions and produces a smooth gentle response.

Some cruise control systems may use an actuator unit comprising an electric motor with integral gearing and electromagnetic clutch. The rotary motion is converted into linear motion with the clutch, a selector gear and a lever.

Electronic anti-lock braking systems

Anti-lock brake systems (sometimes called anti-skid systems), through constant monitoring of wheel speeds, intermittently regulate brake fluid pressures to prevent the brakes from locking-up the wheels and causing the tyres to lose grip, i.e. skid on the road. Fig 8.7 shows block diagrams of an electronic anti-lock system.

When the wheel speed decreases rapidly, a wheel speed sensor detects the condition and the control unit intermittently actuates a solenoid pressure controller, effectively turning the brake fluid pressure to that wheel off and on. The reduced brake pressure prevents the wheel from locking.

Basic principle of operation

The basic system shown in block diagram form in Fig 8.7(a) shows that each 'braked' assembly has a sensor which constantly monitors the rotational speed of the road wheel. This sensor generates an electrical signal and sends a stream of pulses to the electronic control unit (ECU). These sensor signals are constantly monitored and compared with the other wheel speed signals by the electronic devices in the ECU.

If during braking lock-up of one wheel becomes imminent the sensor signal from that wheel will differ from the sensor signals from the other road wheels. The ECU reads this difference in speed and outputs another electrical signal to the pressure control actuator to reduce the hydraulic pressure to the affected wheel. Constant adjustment (pumping) of the hydraulic pressure at the affected wheel is maintained until the ECU interprets the same rate of deceleration (same wheel speeds) by all the sensed wheels (Fig 8.7(b)).

A warning lamp system is included to indicate when the brakes are under the control of the ECU and to monitor brake fluid level and actuator pressure.

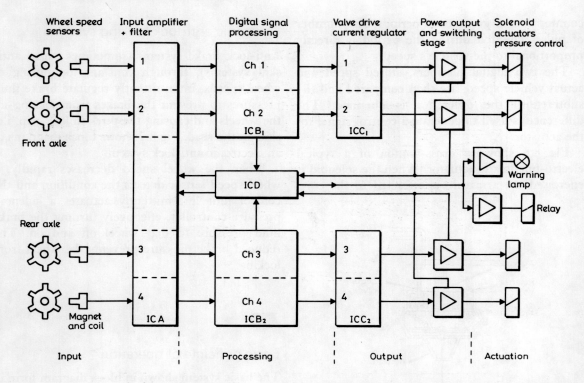

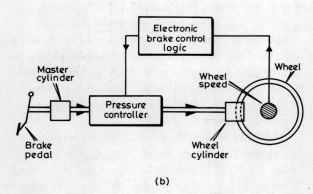

(b)

Fig 8.7   Typical electronic anti-lock braking system
(a) Block diagram of whole system
(b) Block diagram of a single wheel showing feedback
control

Anti-skid braking system (single line)

In this system only the rear braking pressure is electronically controlled (Fig 8.8).

The wheel speed sensor is located on the rear axle housing and is positioned close to the toothed reluctor ring mounted on the revolving pinion shaft-flange. A magnetic field within the sensor is interrupted by the variable reluctance of the toothed reluctor ring, producing an electrical pulse whose frequency is related to speed.

If there are 45 'teeth' on the reluctor ring a signal every 8 degrees ($360/45 = 8$) will be generated by the sensor. This ac signal varies in frequency and amplitude according to the rotational speed of the reluctor. The sensor gap is very precise and care must be taken to ensure the sensor mounting faces are clean and not damaged or distorted. The sensor is also magnetic and precautions should be taken to ensure it is not subjected to demagnetising conditions.

Under normal driving conditions the actuator solenoid valve is switched off. In the off position the actuator pressurisation spring, via the piston and plunger, holds the fluid-pressure cut-ball off its seat, allowing brake fluid under pressure from the brake master cylinder to be applied to the rear wheel cylinders in the normal way, without interruption.

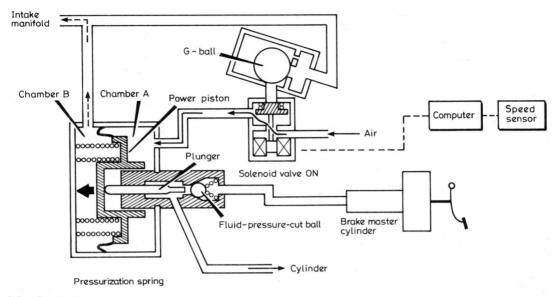

Fig 8.8   *Single line actuator operation*

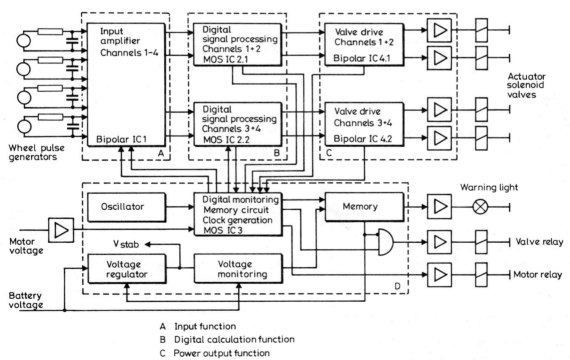

A   Input function
B   Digital calculation function
C   Power output function
D   Monitoring and safety function

Fig 8.9   *Block diagram of an electronic control unit*

vy braking conditions or when the
eration is more than 1 g (9.8 ms^{-2}),
accelerated down the ramp closing
port, connected to the inlet manifold.
The ECU, having sensed a significant change in
wheel speed, outputs a control signal to the solenoid actuator valve, which opens allowing atmospheric air pressure to enter chamber A of the
actuator. The increase in air pressure forces the
power piston to move against the pressurising
spring, in the direction of the arrow. This action
allows the cut-ball to seat on the valve face and
cut the brake fluid pressure being applied to the
rear brake wheel cylinders. This action maintains
the current level of braking pressure in the rear
brake line to continue the present braking effort,
and prevent the rear brakes from locking.

The frequency of the signal from the ECU
controls the period of pressure difference between
chambers A and B, and hence the cycle of
hydraulic pressure adjustment.

The anti-skid control is applied to the rear
wheels only because they are more likely to lock
during heavy braking, due to the weight transfer,
from rear to front, unloading the rear wheels and
reducing adhesion.

Anti-lock braking system (ABS)

The majority of cars use a dual-circuit (two-line)
braking system, where the front brakes are on a
separate hydraulic circuit to the rear brakes.

With ABS as part of the braking system three-
and four-line hydraulic systems are in common
use, to give independent wheel braking under
anti-lock control.

In a four-line system each of the four braked
wheels has a separate and independent hydraulic
fluid pressure pipeline, whereas in the three-line
system the two rear brakes share a hydraulic fluid
pressure pipeline, and possibly a common speed
sensor as in the anti-skid system. There are variants which measure the rear wheel speed inde-
pendently, even though they share the same pipeline.

In one system the front brakes are activated by
a single piston master cylinder and the rear brakes
by controlled accumulator pressure. Another system utilises a dual piston master cylinder for front
and rear brake operations, and an electrical return
pump to feed the brake fluid which is released by
the wheel brake cylinder during pressure reduction back into the appropriate brake circuit. The
return pump is of the double piston type in order
that the dual-circuit braking system remains fully
isolated from each other.

Electronic control unit

Signals from the wheel speed sensors are evaluated
by the ECU which then computes the permissible
wheel slip for optimum braking. It controls the
fluid pressure in the wheel cylinders via solenoid
valves in the actuator.

At the start of a journey, the system will automatically carry out a self check of all the functions
in accordance with a stored programme. The system is continually monitored during a journey
and if any system or component is not operating
satisfactorily the anti-lock part of the braking system is shut down and the system reverts to a non-
anti-lock system. A warning lamp is used to alert
the driver that the anti-lock system is non-oper-
ational.

The ECU is a complex unit, comprising some
seven ICs of the latest digital technology, on which
many demands are made. For the purpose of
explaining the ECU's functional operation these
can be divided into four functional areas.

1 Input – amplifying and signal conditioning
   (ICA).
2 Computing – digital signal processing (ICB).
3 Output – valve drive and power stage (ICC).
4 Safety – monitoring and fault detection (ICD).

Fig 8.9 shows a block diagram of the basic construction of the ECU.

Input section

In this section the electrical signals from the four
wheel-speed sensors are fed through for filtering

and amplification. The input interface usually uses bipolar technology, and the input amplifier is provided with special interference suppression and self-test circuitry.

Computing section

The heart of the controller is formed by the two digital LSI circuits, with each employing two channels for processing the signals and executing the logic process. Some 16,000 transistors are accommodated on a chip area of approximately 37 mm². Silicon gate N–channel technology is used and the controllers are custom designed for this task.

The digital controller, which is similar in design to a microprocessor, contains special computing modules. These modules are better suited to the ABS task than microprocessors, at this stage of development, especially with regard to computing speed and accuracy.

A digital phase lock loop circuit is used to measure the speed of two wheels, filter the signal and convert it into a digital word. A serial arithmetic unit then calculates the wheel slip and the wheel deceleration or acceleration which are then integrated in the following logic circuit to form command signals for the actuator valves in order to obtain brake pressure modulation.

The slip value is obtained by comparing the vehicle speed with the speed of wheel rotation. An optimum braking force which gives 8–30% slip is used as a reference value for vehicle speed. This vehicle reference speed is derived from each of the diagonally opposed wheels. The two wheel speeds are processed by two separate digital modules which are then compared in turn to give a vehicle reference speed. This speed value is used in the logic circuits as if it were the vehicle's road speed.

Output section

When all the relevant signals and/or information has been processed the output section is used to send commands to the solenoid valves, in the actuator assembly, by energising the respective relays.

The output section uses current regulators within the valve drive ICs. By way of these current regulators the output signals from the logic circuit cause different currents to flow in the power output stages. With the result that the desired positional operation of the solenoid valve is obtained.

Under ABS braking on road surfaces with different friction coefficients, left and right, some vehicles may experience a yawing moment which is difficult for the driver to control. The yawing moment causes a sideways movement of the vehicle due to a torque acting about the vertical axis of the vehicle. To counteract this the output drive signals for the solenoid valves on the steering axle are processed so as to reduce the build up of these yawing moments. This is done by using an algorithm that produces a drive signal for the solenoid valve of the front wheel with the higher friction coefficient that delays the build up of braking pressure to the optimum required for retardation. The gain in stability is paid for with longer stopping distances.

The amplifying and filtering, differentiating and calculating wheel slip, deriving the commands for the actuators and outputting them takes approximately 0.5 ms.

Each of the functional areas described above which makes up the digital controller (computer) contains a monitoring circuit for the detection of faults.

Monitoring and safety section

The basic function of this section is to detect any incorrect electrical or electronic signals. The section uses a digital monitoring circuit, a voltage monitor, a voltage regulator, a fault memory with relay and lamp driver.

A fault signal from the monitoring circuits sets the fault memory and switches off the system via the cut-off relay and the voltage regulator. The driver is informed by means of the warning lamp that the control is inoperative and that normal braking is available 'failed safe'.

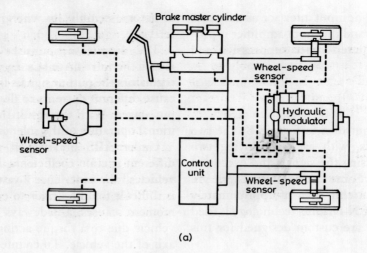

(a)

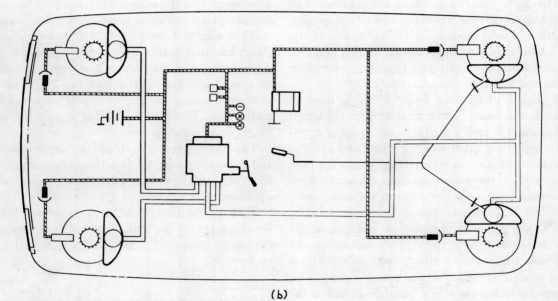

(b)

Fig 8.10   Electronic antilock braking systems
(a) With hydraulic modulation assembly
(b) With actuator assembly

The safety circuit can also transmit a self-test signal to check that all is in working order. The self-test cycle begins when the wheel speed at all the speed channels exceeds 5–7 km/h. After the self-test has verified that the system is in good order, the warning light goes out.

Another function of the safety circuit is to monitor the battery voltage and if the voltage falls below a pre-set value, the ABS will be shut down. The system will be restored when the voltage rises above the pre-set value again.

This ensures that the battery's state of charge does not affect the value of current flowing through the solenoid windings, and hence valve position, when the ABS is in operation.

Actuator

There are two types of actuator assemblies in common use, one is a separate assembly to the brake master cylinder unit (hydraulic modulator assembly) (Fig 8.10(a)) and the other is integral with the master cylinder (actuation assembly) (Fig. 8.10(b)).

Hydraulic modulator assembly

The hydraulic modulator consists of a solenoid valve and accumulator for each brake line, a return pump and the control relays.

The solenoid valves are actuated by the ECU and depending on the driving signal's control current and switching state they connect the wheel cylinder with the brake master cylinder or the electrical return pump. They can also close off the wheel cylinder from both circuits and the pump.

Pre-tensioned springs are located on the armature of the solenoid valve to limit the armature movements during the different control currents. The solenoid valves increase, hold steady or decrease the brake line fluid pressure between 4 and 10 times per second depending upon the state of the road conditions.

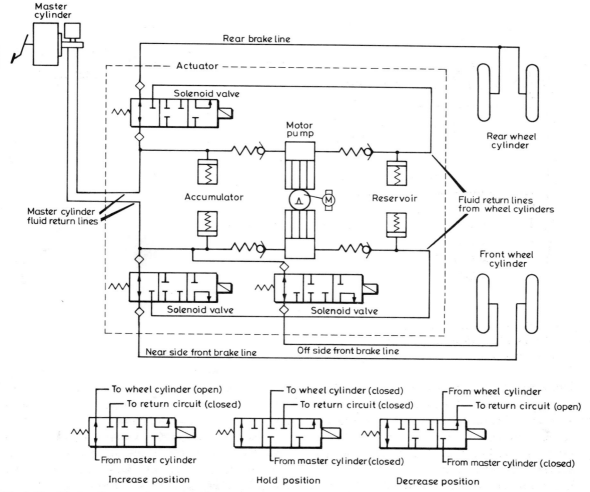

Fig 8.11   *Hydraulic control circuit diagram*

When the pressure is reduced, the return pump pumps the brake fluid released from the wheel cylinders back to the appropriate circuit of the brake master cylinder, by way of an accumulator. The accumulator, temporarily, stores the fluid from the wheel cylinder which occurs following a drop in line pressure. Whenever time line depressurisation takes place a back pressure is produced in the master cylinder fluid line which causes the brake pedal to raise slightly. Because of this the functional operation of the ABS can be felt by the pulsing of the brake pedal as the pressure in the master cylinder fluid lines is cycled on and off.

Principle of operation

When braking with an ABS the ECU's output signal has three different conditions to control the position of the solenoid valve. Under these conditions the following pressures positions are involved:

- Pressure increasing position (normal brake condition).
- Maintained or pressure hold position.
- Pressure decreasing position.

Fig 8.11 shows a schematic line diagram of a hydraulic modulator controlling three brake lines, and as can be seen there are as many actuating solenoids as there are brake lines. In a four line system there would be four of these solenoid valves – one for each wheel cylinder.

Increase pressure position

During normal braking, fluid from the master cylinder flows through the solenoid valves to the wheel cylinders. The wheel speed sensors have not transmitted any abnormal or rapid deceleration signal to the ECU. Consequently, no actuating current will be supplied to the solenoid valves, and the armature spring holds the valve in the 'at-rest' position.

Hold pressure position

When a wheel-speed sensor signals a high rate of

wheel deceleration or the ECU detects that the wheel rotation is out of phase with the other wheel, due to heavy braking or different frictional surfaces, and the wheels are likely to lock. To prevent this the braking pressure at the wheel(s) concerned is initially kept constant. This is achieved by the ECU outputting a signal to the appropriate power transistor which in turn allows battery current to be supplied to the solenoid winding.

The current supplied causes the valve to move to a position that closes both the inlet and outlet ports and the braking system is in the hold phase, and the valve in the hold position.

Decrease pressure position

If the wheel rotation continues to decelerate at an abnormal rate, the ECU will then, via the current regulators, allow an increase in current to flow through the solenoid winding, moving the armature still further and open the port to the return pump. The pressure in the wheel cylinder is reduced so that the wheel is not braked excessively.

At the same time the motor relay is closed by another ECU's signal so that the motor pump can operate and draw fluid from the wheel cylinder via the accumulator. The pump then transfers the fluid to the master cylinder fluid line against the pressure applied to the brake pedal.

When the wheel rotational speed accelerates again the ECU having processed the sensor signals will cause the pump motor to be switched off and move the solenoid valve to the increased position permitting the fluid pressure to be restored. This cycle of operation between the three positions takes place between 4 and 10 times every second the ABS is in operation.

The actuator relay for the solenoid valves is always energised (closed) by an ECU signal whenever the system operates, except in the case of a fault (Fig 8.12).

The fault detecting circuit is always monitoring the system operations and produces the fault signal for the failsafe circuit whenever faults occur.

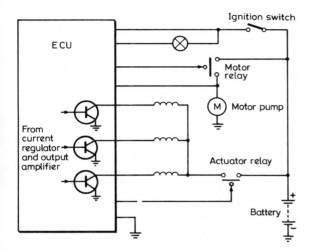

Fig 8.12 Electrical control circuit

The failsafe circuit opens the actuator relay and switches the failure indicator lamp on.

When used, at this stage of development, the self diagnosis display consists of 8 light-emitting-diodes mounted on the surface of the ECU. Each LED turns on according to the fault signal to give a visual indication of what components have malfunctioned.

Actuation assembly

This type of ABS actuation assembly contains a number of interactive components (Fig 8.13).

1 Integral brake fluid *reservoir*.
2 *Reservoir warning unit*, used to indicate when the brake fluid level is low and to switch the ABS control off in the event of low fluid level.
3 *Electric pump*, an electric pump is used to draw fluid from the reservoir and send it at high pressure to the lower region of the accumulator. The pump is of the double piston type so that the brake circuit of the dual-line system remain fully isolated from each other.
4 *Accumulator*, the pressure accumulator has a gas filled chamber behind a flexible diaphragm. As the pump continues to supply fluid to one side of the diaphragm, the nitrogen gas on the other side is compressed so that a

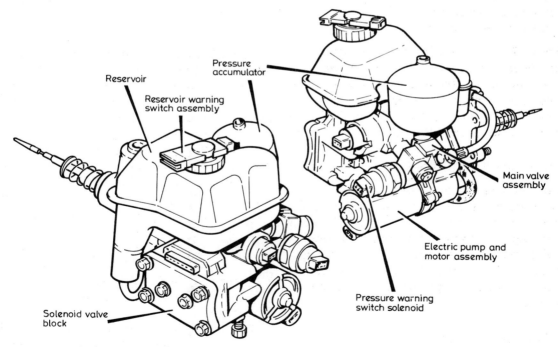

Fig 8.13 Hydraulic actuator assembly

reservoir of brake fluid under high pressure is established.

5 *Pressure switch*, this is used to monitor the pressure in the accumulator so that the pump can be switched on and off. When the pressure reaches a maximum threshold of 180 bar the pump is switched off. When the pressure falls below 140 bar the pump is switched on again. Should the pressure fall below 105 bar the pressure switch acts as a safety device signalling the ECU to switch the ABS system off, and illuminate the warning lamps.

6 *Main valve*, this electromagnetic switching valve is used to open the connecting channel between the pressure region of the brake power booster and the pressure region in front of the master cylinder, and to close the flow of fluid to the reservoir during ABS control. This ensures a continuous supply of high pressure brake fluid during ABS control. When the ABS is not in operation the main valve is closed by the ECU and the return to the reservoir is reopened.

7 *Valve block*, the valve block contains six solenoid valves, two for each brake line. These are used as the inlet and outlet valves for the flow of brake fluid. Under normal braking the valves are in the 'at rest' position where the inlet solenoid valve is open and the outlet solenoid valve is closed. With the brake fluid pressure being applied to the wheel cylinder through the inlet valve when the brakes are applied.

When abnormal deceleration of a wheel(s) occurs the ECU closes the inlet valve and opens the outlet valve. So reducing the brake line pressure and preventing the wheel(s) from locking. To achieve an even and controlled deceleration of the vehicle the two valves are cycled on and off by the ECU at approximately 12 times per second.

In the case of a fault in the system the solenoid valves are not activated by the ECU so that the normal braking function is available.

Principle of operation

As with the modulator type, the actuation assembly is controlled by different output signals to provide alternative operating conditions (Fig 8.14).

Normal brake operation

When the brake pedal is pushed down the control valve is moved to open and fluid under pressure from the accumulator is made available in the boost chamber. The value of the fluid pressure being proportional to the amount of control valve movement. This booster pressure acts on the brake power booster piston (12) and via the open inlet solenoid valve (13) provides the braking pressure for the rear wheel cylinders. At the same time the master cylinder piston (4) displaces brake fluid and builds up the pressure in the brake lines to the front wheel cylinder, again via the open inlet valves in their brake lines.

Throughout this condition the outlet valves stay closed preventing any ABS action.

ABS controlled brake operation

The ABS control comes into operation when the deceleration of one or more road wheels show abnormal deceleration and the associated tendency to lock. Under these conditions the ECU switches on the output transistor to close the electrical circuit of the inlet solenoid, which moves the solenoid's armature piston to the closed position preventing any more fluid getting to the wheel cylinder. At first the pressure in the line is kept constant (hold position) with both the inlet and outlet valves being closed. If the wheel continues to decelerate a second signal from the ECU opens the outlet valve, decreasing the pressure, reducing the braking efforts and returning the 'excess' fluid to the reservoir.

As soon as the system enters the anti-lock mode the main hydraulic solenoid valve (5) is opened by an electrical signal from the ECU. This allows boost pressure to enter the master cylinder area

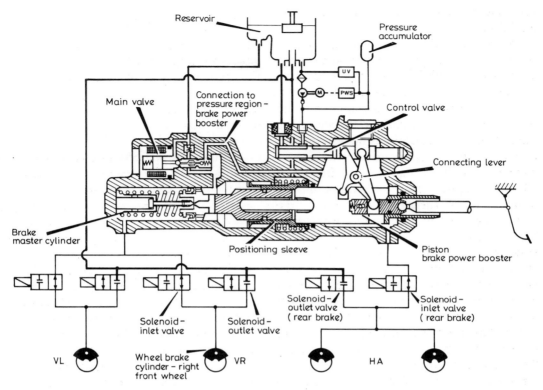

Fig 8.14   Hydraulic control diagram

by flowing in the reverse direction and over its seal. The front brakes now become dynamically powered the same as the rear brakes. The main valve stays open and the inlet and outlet continue to cycle on and off adjusting the brake pressure until the wheel sensors indicate equal braking on all four wheels.

The reason for opening the main solenoid valve is to ensure that there is an adequate supply of high pressure fluid, even under prolonged ABS braking, is available to compensate for the fluid released from the wheel cylinder back to the reservoir.

Because this type of actuator operates at a high working pressure (180 bar), the system must be depressurised before any work is done on the system. The system can be depressurised by pumping the brake pedal some 20 times until the pedal feels hard.

The front brakes can be bled in the normal way,

but the rear brakes can only be bled using the system's own pressure.

Summary of the control sequence

With reference to Fig 8.15, when a wheel speed sensor signals a high rate of deceleration such that the wheels are likely to lock, the electronic controller acts to prevent any further increase in

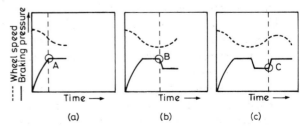

Fig 8.15   Graphs showing the variation in braking pressure under controlled braking

braking pressure. The braking pressure of the wheel(s) concerned is initially kept constant (point A), and prevented from increasing.

If the wheel continues to decelerate abnormally, the pressure in the wheel cylinder is reduced so that the braking effort is reduced (point B).

The wheel will then accelerate again due to the reduced pressure. Once a specific threshold has been reached the fluid pressure is increased again (point C), causing the wheel to decelerate, and the control cycle repeats again at a frequency of between 4 and 10 seconds depending on the condition of the road surface.

Microcomputer based control system

The electronic control unit includes the microcomputer components, fault detecting mechanism, failsafe circuits and self diagnosis circuitry.

The microcomputer calculates the wheel rotation speed from the input pulse signal frequency. Evaluation of the wheel rotational situation produces the output signal to prevent the wheel from skidding wherever slip is detected.

As with the previous system the microcomputer's output signal has three different conditions.

1   output signal controls the activating solenoid valve in the pressure increase position for normal braking.
2   pressure hold signal.
3   pressure decrease signal.

The fault detecting mechanism is always monitoring the system's operation and produces the fault signal for failsafe circuit whenever a fault occurs.

The self diagnosis mechanism consists of 6 eight LEDS on the ECU surface. Each LED turns on according to the fault to give a visual indication of the faulty components.

Electronic suspension systems

When a vehicle corners, the force accelerating it towards the centre of turn acts at ground level, but the centre of mass of the vehicle is some distance above ground level. Weight transfer causes the vehicle to lean outwards on its springs, which results in an interaction with the steering linkage and changes the camber angles of the tyres. Energy is stored in the springs, which must be dissipated by the dampers as the vehicle leaves the corner. The moment of inertia of the vehicle about the roll axis and the role stiffness govern the resonant frequency of the suspension system. If the dampers are ineffective or if the vehicle is high and heavy, the roll resonance can turn it over (Fig 8.16). At constant speeds vehicle weight is

Fig 8.16   Body roll when cornering

distributed evenly (Fig 8.17(a)), but during heavy braking, deceleration or acceleration weight is transferred to the front or rear wheels (Fig. 8.17(b)), which affects vehicle safety, ride, handling and comfort. Yet the car must give the driver a good ride on a smooth surface, it has to handle well in corners, and it has to give a reasonable ride on a rough road. Conventional suspension systems are a compromise design not fully satisfying every one of those conditions.

Electronically controlled suspension systems have been developed which can fully satisfy every

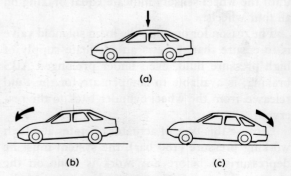

Fig 8.17   Suspension and handling
(a)   Even distribution
(b)   Dive when braking
(c)   Squat on acceleration

one of the above conditions, by manual or automatic selection. The suspension design is based on active suspension principles.

As Fig 8.18(a) shows, an active suspension system interposes hydraulic rams between springs and body and the wheel position is monitored with a sensor. If the wheel moves towards the body, the movement is sensed and causes the ram to extend until the wheel is back in the original position, which compresses the spring. When a vehicle is cornering as in Fig 8.17(b) one spring

will become compressed and the other extended, and the vehicle is prevented from experiencing body roll. Active suspension systems can be implemented by mechanical or hydro-pneumatic means, but as the complexity rises electronic control is the most effective way.

Electronic control unit

An electronically controlled suspension system, illustrated in Fig 8.19, uses a microprocessor-based control unit to adjust the damping force of the four shock absorbers. Table 8.1 lists the main components of the system and their functions and locations.

The control unit adjusts the system such that two levels of damping take place, switched automatically depending on the driving conditions:

- soft – normal driving conditions, eg constant speed on a level, straight road, or slow and steady acceleration or deceleration, slow speed town driving

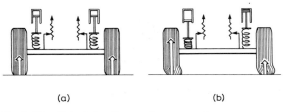

(a)   (b)

Fig 8.18 Principle of an active suspension system
(a) Active suspension interposes rams between springs and body
(b) When vehicle corners, rams counteract weight transfer

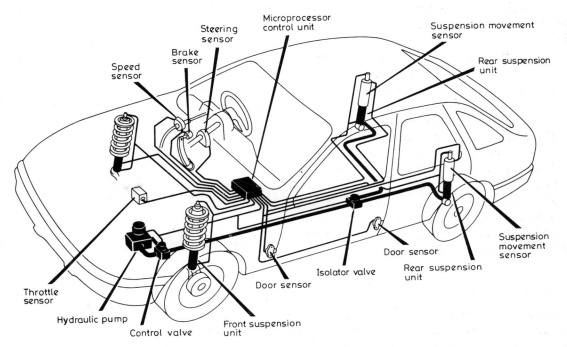

Fig 8.19 Adaptive suspension system with electronic control

Table 8.1   Main components and their functions

Name of component	Function	Location
Shock absorber	Incorporates 2-way switching valve to change damping force	Front and rear suspensions
Actuator	Drives 2-way valve of shock absorber	At top of shock absorber
Mode select switch	Switches the damping force mode	At right of steering column on instrument panel
Mode indicator lamp	Indicates damping force selected	In the meter
Suspension control computer	Controls the system depending on the selected mode	Inside left quarter-panel
Ignition switch	Supplies power to suspension control computer when turned on	Steering column
Steering sensor	Detects steering direction and angle of the steering wheel turn	Bottom of the steering column
Stop lamp switch	Sends braking signal to the computer	Brake pedal bracket
Throttle position sensor	Sends degree of accelerator pedal depression to computer	Throttle body
Car speed sensor	Sends car speed signal to computer	In the meter
Neutral start switch (A/T only)	Sends P (parking) and N (neutral) range signals to computer	Transmission

- hard – harsh or sports driving conditions, eg cornering at speed, hard acceleration or deceleration, high speed

When the system switches from soft to hard damping, the spring constant increases by about 50% and the damping coefficient increases by about 150%. The driver has the option to override automatic control, and switch permanently to either of these two damping settings.

The five sensors around the vehicle allow the control unit to monitor vehicle speed, rate at which the steering wheel turns, acceleration or deceleration, throttle operating rate, and suspension stroke. A change in driving conditions causes the monitored signals to change and, if the signal change is sufficient, the control unit switches the suspension accordingly.

Acceleration sensor

The acceleration sensors are of the pendulum-type detecting acceleration changes in three directions: longitudinal, lateral, and vertical. The pendulum sensor, due to its pivot and weight arrangement,

has independent threshold sensitivities in the three directions:

1   longitudinal – over 0.3 g
2   lateral – over 0.5 g
3   vertical – over 1.0 g.

A light beam between a source and detector detects pendulum movement: when the beam is broken, the pendulum has exceeded one or more of the threshold sensitivities and the control unit switches to hard suspension mode, to counteract the accelerating force.

Steering sensor

The steering wheel sensor is an angular velocity sensor, which allows the control unit to monitor the rate of change of steering wheel angle. A slotted disc rotated by the steering mechanism separately interrupts two infra-red beams: The angular velocity is determined by the control-unit from the difference in time between the first beam interruption and the second. When the steering wheel angular velocity exceeds a threshold the control unit switches to its hard suspension mode, so that greater damping force is automatically provided to, say, prevent rolling when cornering or give easier handling when pulling out to overtake.

Suspension stroke sensor

The suspension stroke sensor uses photo interrupters to monitor the relative positions between the body and suspension. The control unit monitors the sensor signals and changes the suspension to hard mode if it determines that either the upper or lower limits of the suspension stroke are approached. This helps prevent the incidence of full bump and/or full rebound.

Vehicle speed sensor

Located in the transmission or speedometer cable, this sensor is a typical inductive pick-up, and provides a train of pulses whose frequency is proportional to vehicle speed.

The control unit monitors the speed and automatically switches to hard suspension mode at speeds above 120 km/h.

Throttle speed sensor

The throttle speed sensor is used to detect the speed at which the accelerator pedal is being operated. It may take the form of a pedal pressure sensor or a simple potentiometric sensor. When the sensor signals indicate that the throttle movement speed (accelerating or decelerating) is over preset threshold limits, the control unit automatically switches to hard suspension mode, so as to maintain a more level vehicle condition under acceleration or deceleration.

Actuators

There are two main types of activator/damper arrangements available. The first has a damper with a twin-chamber construction, whose oil passages between the two cylinders may be opened and closed to give soft and hard damping (Fig

8.20(a)). The oil passage orifices are located in a rotary valve, which is integrated with the control rod driven by the actuator. Under normal, soft driving conditions the control rod opens the valve orifices, allowing a greater flow of oil between the

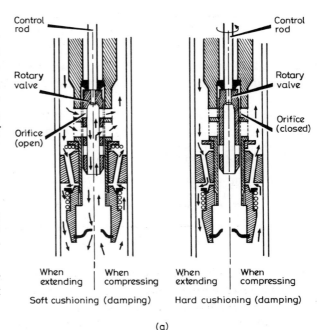

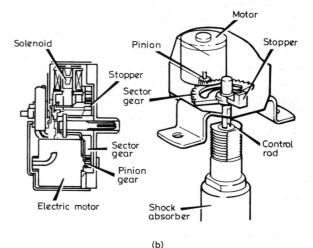

Fig 8.20 Twin-chamber electrically actuated suspension damper
(a) *Construction of damper*
(b) *Construction of actuator*

top and bottom chambers. In the hard sports mode the control rod closes the valve preventing oil flow. The dampers resemble large diameter ordinary suspension dampers and are normally installed in the same place as conventional vehicle dampers.

The actuator used to drive the rotary valve is a permanent magnet DC motor (Fig 8.20(b)). The DC motor is controlled directly by the control unit, taking approximately 0.1 s to actuate, thus providing a fairly rapid change in suspension mode.

The second type of actuator/damper arrangement is described by its manufacturer, Lotus, as a synthetic electronic spring. The actuator is, in fact, a hydraulic ram powered by a small engine driven pump and controlled by varying the volume of oil in the actuators (via a servo valve). The system is inherently self-levelling and can be controlled to eliminate roll in corners and to be exceptionally soft or hard. The hydraulic actuator also replaces the road springs, dampers and anti-roll bars.

Fig 8.21 shows the Lotus active ride suspension system and the electro–hydraulic suspension dampers in detail.

A mode lamp is normally provided in active electronic suspension systems to indicate whether the damping force is set soft or hard. When a failure occurs, an alarm light is also used to inform the driver of the malfunction and of the measures taken by the control unit (eg fixed to hard mode). Data regarding the malfunction are provided on a harness check terminal as coded signals to help diagnosis of failure.

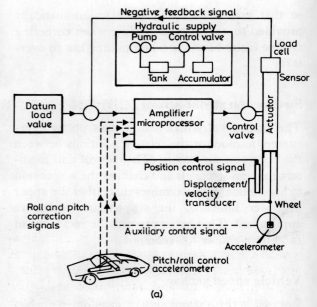

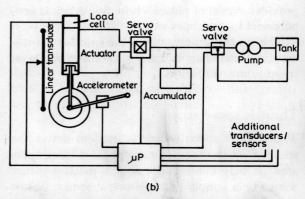

Fig 8.21   *The Lotus active ride suspension system*
(a) *Principle*
(b) *Block diagram*

9

Total management systems

The trend towards more advanced and more integrated engine control systems has resulted in total management systems, combining ignition, fuelling function, automatic transmission and other key engine functions into a single centralised engine management and control system. Rightly so: such systems afford many advantages; fully optimised engine performance and lower overall cost from the use of common components being only two. A single microprocessor, single power supply and single housing are used in a single control unit – rather than having separate control units each with microprocessor, supply and housing, for each function. Common sensors are used to provide input signals, too.

Total electronic management control systems (TEMCS) provide highly integrated and precise control of engine and transmission functions through the use of a common microprocessor-based computer. Precision control is achieved not only for engine idling speed, fuel injection volume, and ignition timing, but also the computer link-up with an automatic transmission system means optimum gear-changing points and control of lock-up clutch operation, so providing a more efficient transmission of power, improved driving performance and higher fuel economy.

TEMCS are designed to combat the increasing complexity of today's engines and strict emission legislation. They also have an advanced self-diagnostic capability for the instant detection of a malfunction; together with fail-safe and self-repair

functions which help the vehicle to continue to operate even in the event of a fault. Fig 9.1(a) shows a block diagram of the TEMCS principle and Fig 9.1(b) illustrates a typical system. Although most control categories have been discussed in earlier chapters, a brief description of each category follows.

Electronic fuel injection (EFI)

Electronic fuel injection (Fig 9.2) is based on the intermittent fuel injection principle; using sensor signals and data maps stored in an electronic memory to compute the optimum injection timing and fuel discharge duration. The fuel is discharged exactly to the engine's various operating conditions of: cold starting; warm-up phase; idling; part-load; full-load; acceleration; deceleration; air density; battery voltage fluctuation; fuel pump control.

Electronic ignition control

The TEMCS control unit is programmed with data to provide optimum ignition characteristics (Fig 9.3) under all operating conditions. Many features are included: ignition triggering; spark advance and retard; constant coil energy; variable dwell periods; ignition advance under idling conditions; knock control allowing the ignition point to be set for maximum torque at full load without knocking.

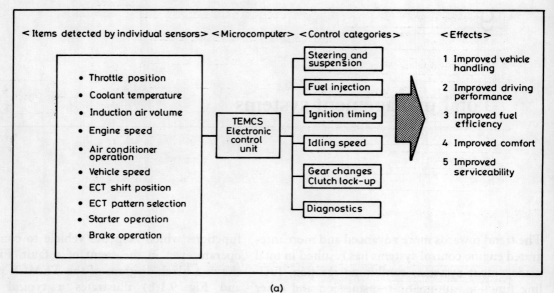

(a)

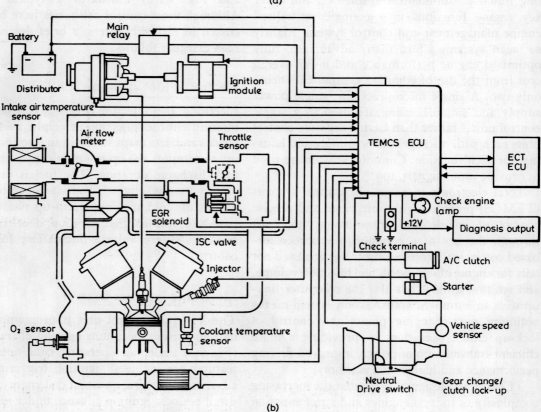

(b)

Fig 9.1   Total electronic management control systems
(a) Block diagram
(b) Typical TEMCS

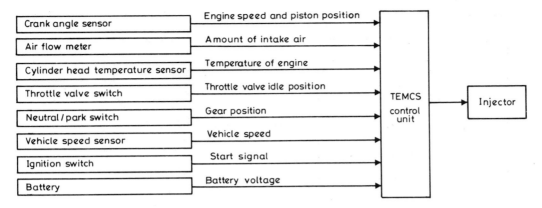

Fig 9.2   Electronic fuel injection

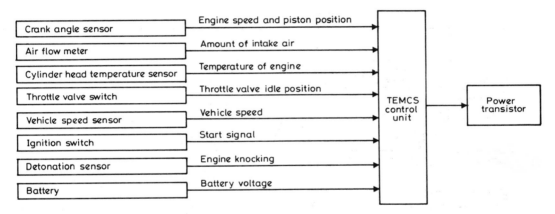

Fig 9.3   Electronic ignition timing control

The last feature also allows the ignition point to run close to the engine's knock threshold, and retards the ignition should the threshold be breached. Knock in turbo-charged engines can also be prevented by reducing boost pressure and retarding the ignition timing as soon as knock is detected.

Speed control

The control unit is programmed with target engine speed values to respond to different engine condition and operating requirements (Fig 9.4). Via the idle speed actuator, the control unit adjusts idle speed to the target value. Also, fuel injection pulses are suppressed to limit the engine speed to a preset maximum. A TEMCS may also provide cruise control features.

Electronic accelerator

An integrated potentiometer is attached to the accelerator pedal to provide information on the pedal's position to the control unit. This is used in conjunction with data from other sensors to calculate the optimum throttle butterfly valve position and so set the throttle actuator. The use of an electronic accelerator eliminates a mechanical source of error due to play, friction and wear.

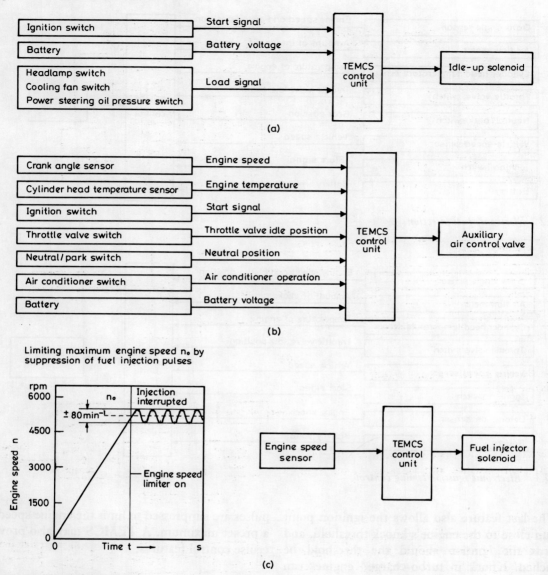

Fig 9.4   *Engine speed control*
(a) *Idle-up control*
(b) *Idle speed control*
(c) *Maximum engine speed control*

Exhaust emissions control

Exhaust gas recirculation (EGR)

In an EGR system, some exhaust gas is returned to the combustion chamber (Fig 9.5), thus lowering the flame temperature during combustion and reducing the nitrogen oxide density in the exhaust gas. When the EGR valve is open, exhaust gas can flow from the exhaust manifold to the intake manifold. The EGR valve is regulated by the control valve (solenoid operated) to govern the amount of exhaust gas that flows.

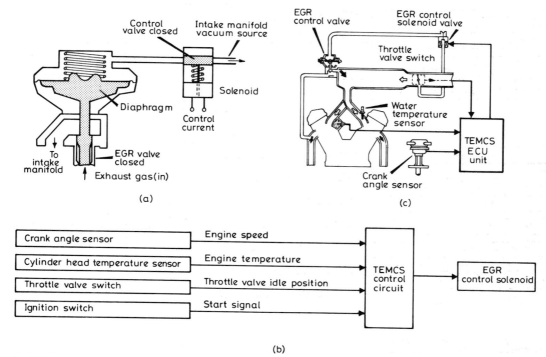

Fig 9.5   *Exhaust gas recirculation control*
(a) *Actuator details*
(b) *Block diagram*
(c) *Layout*

Generally EGR only occurs when the engine is at normal temperature and running at medium speed.

Air-fuel ratio

The air-fuel ratio control circuit regulates the air volume entering the inlet manifold, or the volume of fuel discharged through the injector valves: helping to keep the actual air-fuel ratio close to the stoichiometric (i.e. when $\lambda = 1$) air-fuel ratio. This results in a complete combustion which minimises the production of carbon monoxide (CO) and unburned hydro-carbons (HC).

In an air supply feedback control system, the main air supply enters the inlet manifold from the air filter and carburettor, as in Fig 9.6(a). After combustion a lambda oxygen sensor attached to the exhaust manifold detects the air-fuel ratio in the exhaust, signalling this information to the

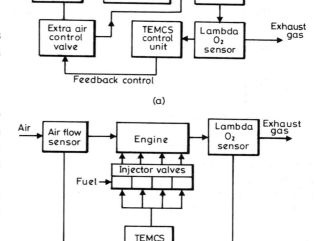

Fig 9.6   *TEMCS control of air-fuel ratio*
(a) *Using an extra air control valve*
(b) *Using fuel injection*

computer. On the basis of this information the control unit adjusts the extra air control valve to maintain the ideal air-fuel ratio. Alternatively, in a fuel injection system the control unit increases or decreases the fuel volume injected (Fig. 9.6(b)) and so maintains the ideal air-fuel ratio.

Electronic transmission control

Electronic transmission control (Fig 9.7), improves fuel economy and gear-change quality, and increases a given transmission torque and reliability. The control unit directly controls the gearbox's pressure regulator, solenoid valves and clutch actuators. Gear-change characteristic curves, stored in memory, are used to effect the best change schedule for fuel economy or power performance.

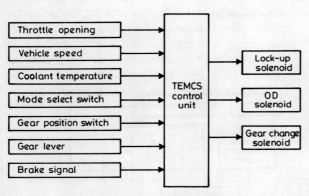

Fig 9.7   *Block diagram transmission control*

Fuel pressure regulator

Electronic control may be added to the fuel injection pressure control circuit, so as to increase fuel pressure and make it easier to start a hot engine. This is achieved by shutting off the manifold vacuum supply to the pressure regulator during starting, and for 3 minutes after starting when the water temperature is above 100°C.

Fig 9.8(a) shows graphically how the pressure regulator normally maintains a constant pressure difference between manifold absolute pressure and fuel pressure, by changing the fuel pressure as

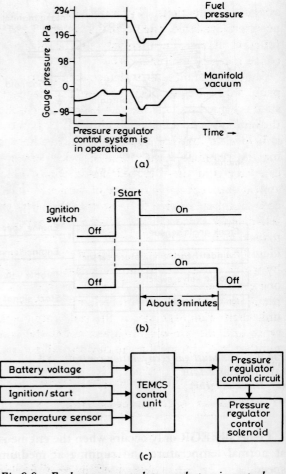

Fig 9.8   *Fuel pressure regulator – electronic control system*
(a) *Showing pressure variations*
(b) *Control pulse*
(c) *Block diagram*

manifold absolute pressure changes. But, when the electronic control system is in operation the fuel pressure is increased, for the duration of the control pulse. Fig 9.8(b) shows the control pulse, while Fig 9.8(c) illustrates the control circuit and system.

Self diagnostics

An on-board diagnostic function is provided in the control unit to detect, memorise and display system malfunctions. Typically, fourteen diagnoses are available, one normal state and 13 malfunction states. The majority of the diagnoses concern sensor malfunctions.

When a system fault is detected an instrument panel warning light is switched on. The diagnosed state is logged into memory and stored, even after the ignition is switched off. This memory function is helpful in locating a problem which otherwise may be extremely hard to find. Service personnel can later read these logged malfunctions which appear as a repeatable display of sequenced error code numbers. Table 9.1, for example, lists the self-diagnosis code in the Nissan ECCS engine management system. The code number needed to identify a fault is determined from the frequency by which two coloured indicator lamps (one red, one green) go on and off. The red lamp refers to the tenth digit while the green lamp refers to the unit digit. For example, if the red lamp blinks twice and the green lamp three times the code number is 23: indicating the throttle valve switch is malfunctioning.

When such self diagnostic systems detect a very abnormal signal, the system may ignore the signal; instead using a predetermined value thus maintaining vehicle operation, albeit now under open loop control.

Vehicle handling management system

As automotive technology advances, chassis and suspension systems are becoming increasingly complex – now with electronic control features helping to provide superior handling and comfort. Working on a similar concept to TEMCS, vehicle handling management systems integrate several control functions into one central electronic control unit. The block diagram in Fig 9.9 shows the concept of such a control system; based on seven input signals and the activation of steering, suspension and antilock braking devices.

Suspension and anti-lock braking systems have already been discussed, but speed responsive rack and pinion steering systems need mention (Fig 9.10). The control unit controls the current in the solenoid valve so that the power-assistance ratio is light at low speeds, heavier at high speeds.

Table 9.1 Self diagnostic error codes in the Nissan ECCS engine management system

Indication method				Error code no.	Malfunction area
The light goes out	Red light	The light goes out	Green light		
4.8 sec	2.4 sec	2.4 sec	2.4 sec		
	●		●	11	Crank angle sensor
	●		●●	12	Air flow meter
	●		●●●	13	Water temperature sensor
	●		●●●●	14	Vehicle speed sensor
	●●		●	21	Ignition signal
	●●		●●●	23	Throttle valve switch
	●●●		●	31	Air conditioner switch (with Nissan air conditioner)
					OK (without Nissan air conditioner)
	●●●		●●	32	'Start' signal
	●●●		●●●●	34	Detonation sensor
	●●●●		●	41	Air temperature sensor
	●●●●		●●●	43	Battery voltage
	●●●●		●●●●	44	OK (with Nissan air conditioner)

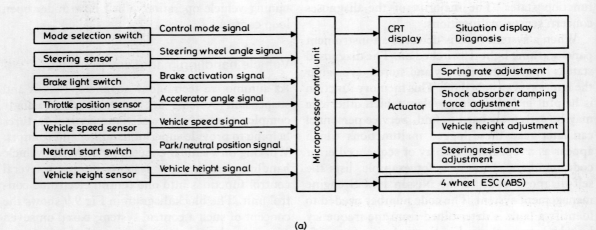

(a)

Fig 9.9   A vehicle handling management system
(a) Block diagram
(b) Hydraulic diagram

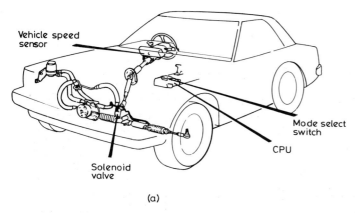

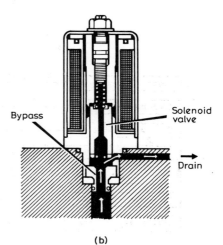

Fig 9.10   Speed responsive power steering
(*a*) *Layout*
(*b*) *Solenoid control valve, varying steering effort
    according to mode and vehicle speed*

10

Electronic control of body systems

You only need sit behind the steering wheel of a modern car and turn on the ignition to see that the micro–chip has arrived: all-electronic dash panels and instrumentation systems are commonplace, with their large and easy to read displays (Fig 10.1). Compared with traditional electro-mechanical instruments, microelectronic displays are able to provide:

- Faster and more accurate information
- increased reliability – there are no moving parts, construction is modular and there are fewer sub-assemblies
- more comprehensive instrumentation while clarity is maintained through flexibility in display area and format, using dotmatrix, alphanumeric, ISO symbols and bargraph displays
- greater freedom in display location for better visibility
- attractive customised displays

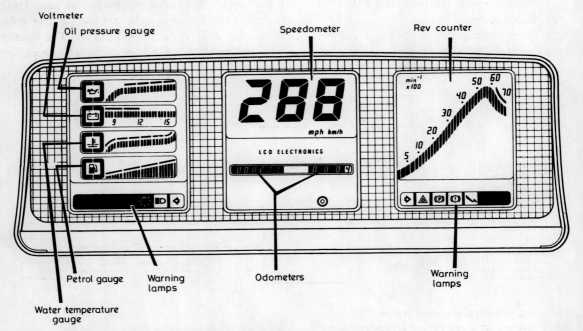

Fig 10.1   Digital electronic instrumentation display panel

- easier accommodation in the dash panel due to shallow depth of electronic panel
- clearer and more extensive instrumentation
- increased vehicle safety, operating efficiency and driver convenience.

Electronic display systems can be separated into active and passive types. Active displays; LED, vacuum fluorescent etc, are triggered, reliable, easy to read and are easy to multiplex. Passive displays such as LCD, have good visibility in strong light, consume very little power even over a large display area.

Driver information and display systems

There have been several changes in the methods of telling the driver what needs to be known about the operating condition of the vehicle:

- combinations of analogue dials with digits
- modular digital dash units
- 'space-age' panels of numbers/bar/graphs, climbing streams of light, coloured warning symbols, and CRT 'television' screens.

There is no denying that it is the colourful displays themselves which have the most appeal; but this is only one factor of an electronic driver information system.

Fig 10.2(a) shows a block diagram of a single information display system. When a microprocessor is used to process signals, however, it may be as the central processor for *several* input signals, and the operation of *several* display devices. Fig 10.2(b) illustrates a typical electronic information display system combining the operations of many instrumentation systems into one.

Digital speedometer (Fig 10.3)

Vehicle speed is monitored by a sensor fitted in the transmission train; usually the gearbox, in place of the more conventional speedometer drive gear (Fig. 10.4(a)). Inside the sensor is a pulse generator, working on induction, Hall effect, or photo–interruption principles, producing 2 to 8 pulses per revolution, up to a maximum speed of about 4,000 rev/min.

The frequency of the generated pulses is proportional to the number of interrupters on the drive rotor and the vehicle speed (Figure 10.4(b)). If the sensor is geared to revolve at say, 1500 rev/mile then for each mile travelled a four pole interrupter will produce 6000 pulses. The sensor signal is conditioned by an interface amplifier

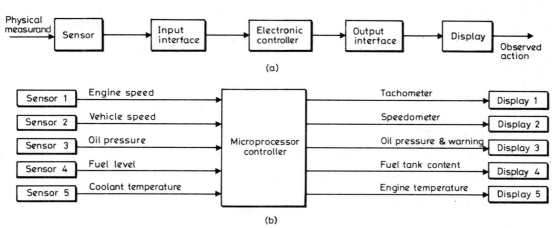

Fig 10.2   *Instrumentation control system*
(a) *Block diagrams of a generalised instrumentation*
(b) *Microprocessor–based instrumentation control system*

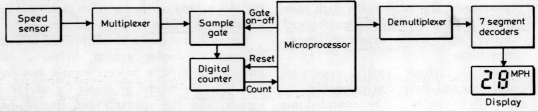

Fig 10.3   *Generalised speedometer electronic instrumentation system*

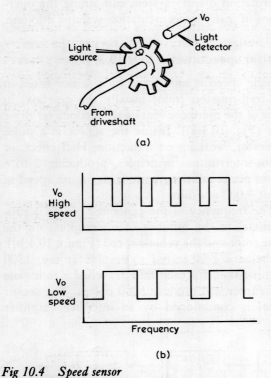

(a)

Fig 10.4   *Speed sensor*
(a) *Typical construction*
(b) *Voltage/frequency characteristic*

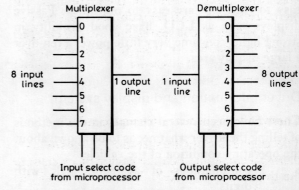

Fig 10.5   *Digital selection devices multiplexer and demultiplexer*

device to a squarewave and sampled (typically) through a multiplexer. The multiplexer is an electronic switching device through which the microprocessor can select one of several sensor inputs for processing. The output is typically switched through a demultiplexer (Fig 10.5). The electronic speedometer operates by counting the number of pulses received from the speed sensor in a given time and from this computes the speed to be displayed. The time slot over which the sensor pulsed signal is counted is controlled directly by the microprocessor, turning on and off a sample gate. After a set of pulses have been counted, the digital counter is reset to zero in readiness for the next count cycle.

After performing necessary computations on the counted number of pulses, the microprocessor indicates the speed on the display.

The display driver circuit selects the display segments to display numerals representing the vehicle's speed, according to the number of pulses received from the speed sensor.

Electronic tachometer

The tachometer operation is similar to the speedometer except that the signal pulses originate from the vehicle ignition system. The number of rev/min of an engine is directly proportional to the sparking frequency and a signal wave-form of this frequency is readily available from the primary ignition coil circuit. After counting these pulses over a fixed time period, the microprocessor

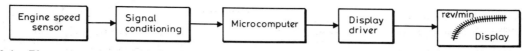

Fig 10.6   Electronic engine speed indicating system (tachometer)

calculates the engine speed and displays the result accordingly; representing the number of 100s of engine revolutions per minute.

For example, a four cylinder, four stroke engine fires twice per revolution of the crankshaft and therefore at, say 6,000 rev/min, the sparking frequency will be 12,000 sparks/min i.e. 200 Hz. The pulses are counted for 0.3s, so the result is '60' hundreds. Fig 10.6 shows an engine speed measurement system.

Coolant temperature measurement

The engine coolant temperature is sensed by a thermistor, mounted on the engine block close to the thermostat (Fig 10.7). The resistance of this sensor decreases with increasing temperature.

Sensor output voltage converted to a binary value by the analogue-to-digital converter, then multiplexed to the microprocessor. The microprocessor uses the binary number to address a particular memory location. Another binary number which corresponds to the actual temperature value for the sensor voltage is stored in that memory location. The microprocessor uses the number from memory to generate the appropriate output signal to activate the display driver circuit to display the temperature value.

If the coolant temperature exceeds a limit then an output signal is generated which activates a warning indicator.

Fuel volume measurement

To measure fuel quantity the microprocessor samples the sensor signal via the analogue-to-digital

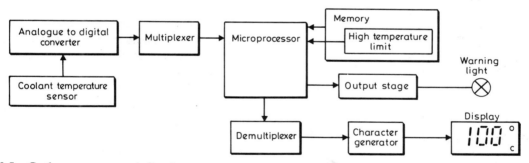

Fig 10.7   Coolant temperature indicating system

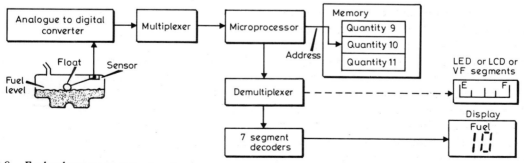

Fig 10.8   Fuel volume measurement system

converter and multiplexer as shown in Fig 10.8, and generates a signal to display the contents of memory at the address indicated. The sensor is a thick-film variable resistance device controlled by a float. The resistor is used as a voltage divider so that the voltage at the caliper arm is related to float position which, in turn, is dependent upon

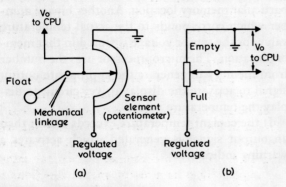

Fig 10.9   Fuel volume sensor
(a) Construction
(b) Circuit

fuel level (Fig 10.9). A table of binary codes equivalent to the fuel volume and the sensor voltage for the fuel tank is stored in ROM.

When the fuel volume level drops to a minimum preset limit the microprocessor also generates an output to activate an audible and/or visual low-fuel warning.

To compensate for fuel movement in the tank the microprocessor samples and stores several readings over a few seconds and computes the average sensor voltage value. The averaged output is used as the memory address for determining the fuel volume value.

Oil pressure measurement

Oil pressure is measured by a piezoresistor sensor (Fig 10.10). A piezoresistor is attached to a diaphragm whose deflection causes a change in the piezoresistor's resistance. The piezoresistor is connected into a simple voltage divider circuit and the voltage across a fixed value resistor is proportional to oil pressure. The analogue sensor voltage is converted to a digital code and used by the microprocessor to address a table of voltage and oil pressure codes stored in ROM. The output signal generated is used to drive the display and thus give a digital representation of the engine oil pressure.

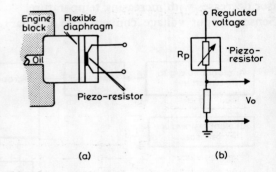

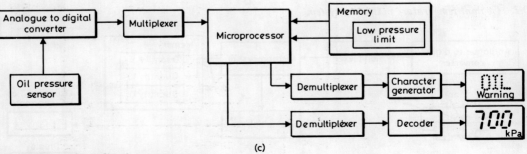

Fig 10.10   Oil pressure indicating system
(a) Sensor details
(b) Circuit of sensor
(c) Oil pressure measurement system

Trip computers

Microprocessor-based trip computers are a major development in vehicle electronics, and with careful use allow more economical driving. A trip computer monitors performance during a journey, displaying a variety of information from fuel consumption to the vehicle's average speed.

For example, press a button and the vehicle's instantaneous fuel consumption is displayed. Or the average fuel consumption since beginning the journey. Or the average speed over the same distance. Or the estimated distance to the next fuel stop; taking into account the way the vehicle has been driven. It may also function as a stopwatch, as well as giving the outside temperature.

Sophisticated trip computers are available which offer some 12 functions, some of which require manual input from the driver or passenger. Key in the desired travel time and the trip distance and the computer will calculate the average speed. Or it can determine the fuel consumption over a particular stretch of road.

Trip computers can be used to help save fuel and make motoring a more enjoyable time.

A block diagram of a trip computer system is shown in Fig 10.11. A diagram showing the trip computer control unit in more detail is shown in Fig 10.12. The trip computer system can either be implemented as a set of special functions of the main microprocessor-based instrumentation system or it can be a stand-alone system employing its own microprocessor.

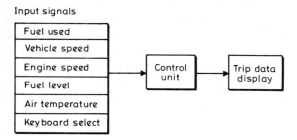

Fig 10.11 Block diagram of trip computer system

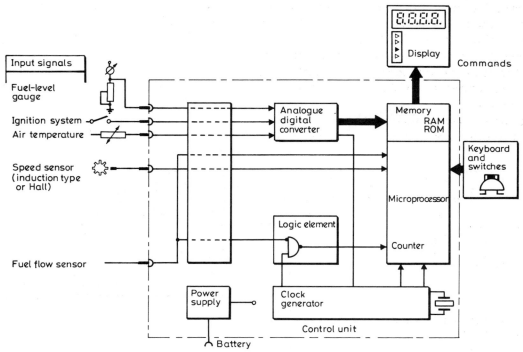

Fig 10.12 Details of trip computer control system

Trip computer operation

The trip computer receives input signals from four sensors, which measure vehicle speed, fuel flow rate, fuel volume and outside air temperature. Using these input signals in conjunction with the internal trip computer clock, a number of functions may typically be calculated and displayed in digital form, all illustrated in Fig 10.13.

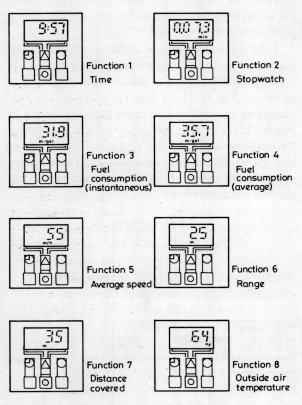

Fig 10.13   Typical trip computer functions

Function 1 – time

The accuracy of a quartz crystal combines with microprocessor technology to provide an easily read display of time regardless of whether the ignition is on or off. The clock may have a 12-hour or 24-hour cycle and is easily reset after the battery or supply has been disconnected. The time is initially entered by pressing the appropriate buttons as specified by the manufacturers.

Function 2 – stopwatch

The stopwatch can be started, stopped and reset to zero using the appropriate button. This elapsed time function can be used for, say, measuring acceleration or finding out how long a journey has taken.

Function 3 – instantaneous fuel consumption

When this function is selected the computer takes a reading of the pulse frequency from the fuel flow sensor i.e. fuel flowing per unit of time. This quantity is used by the computer to determine the fuel consumed per mile or per kilometre and to give an instantaneous consumption display. On fuel injection systems the pulse time is used as a basis for this calculation, which is proportional to the amount of fuel injected. The pulse time of only one injector may be measured, this is then multiplied by the number of cylinders to give the total amount of fuel used. The computer determines the fuel consumption by comparing the fuel flow rate in gallons (litres) per hour to the vehicle speed in miles (kilometres) per hour, defined by:

$$\text{consumption (in mpg)} = \frac{\text{speed (in mph)}}{\text{fuel flow rate (in gph)}}$$

At speeds up to 5 or 6 mph the display may be in gallons per hour; above this preset minimum speed it is in mpg.

The instantaneous fuel consumption is updated frequently, say every second, and as a consequence the display changes rapidly as the operating conditions vary, depending upon accelerator position; cruising, climbing or descending hills, or accelerating etc. By displaying information on the exact amount of fuel being used at any given moment, the trip computer helps driving techniques to be adopted which show useful gains in fuel economy.

Function 4 – average fuel consumption

When the average fuel consumption function is selected the trip computer divides the distance travelled from the start of the trip by the total fuel which has been used.

$$\text{Average fuel consumption} = \frac{\text{distance travelled}}{\text{total fuel}}$$

Both variables are recorded as part of the computer's normal functions; distance travelled is obtained from the speedometer circuit and the fuel used from the fuel flow rate. The calculation can be started and restarted at any time and is not affected if the ignition is switched off. The display shows the figure in mpg or kilometres per litre.

Function 5 – average speed
This value is calculated using the speed pulses, averaged over the time of the journey. The trip computer can show the vehicle's average speed, in mph, at any time during the trip. The function can be restarted at any time, providing useful journey time information for either complete trips or individual sections of a trip. Breaks in the journey with the ignition off are not included.

Function 6 – range
This programme is used to show how far the car is able to travel using the fuel remaining in the tank. The calculation is determined using the contents of the fuel tank and the average fuel consumption. The display shows the distance possible in miles or kilometres.

Function 7 – distance covered
The distance covered since the last reset is calculated by summing the speed pulses derived from the measurement of the vehicle's speed.

Function 8 – outside air temperature
The outside air temperature is measured using the NTC thermistor. The temperature range displayed ranges typically from 40°C to 170°C, and is usually displayed in steps of 0.5°C. Outside air temperature is a source of interesting information for cars fitted with air conditioning. This function can also make a real contribution to road safety; because black ice forms on the road surface at a temperature just above freezing point, and an accurate reading of outside air temperature could give advance warning of black ice conditions.

Trip electronic control unit

The microprocessor used in the trip computer is provided with memories for the various functional programmes, tables and data. Typically, a 32-channel input/output device is provided for communication with the peripheral units, sensors and displays (Fig 10.14). The analogue input quantities are digitized in an analogue-to-digital converter and fed to the microprocessor through a multiplexer. Digital input signals are fed to the microprocessor after filtering by the input devices. Current consumption is kept down to about 5 mA which means that the battery is subjected to only a slight electrical load. It is also because of this low current consumption that continuous realtime operation of the display and control electronics is made possible. Additionally, the system will still function reliably even if the supply voltage falls below 5v.

Display driver circuits are used to generate the characters on the liquid crystal or vacuum fluorescent display. With the LCD type, one of the driver IC contains the oscillator required for generating the alternating voltage.

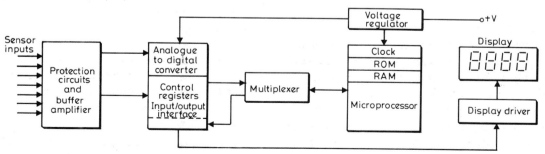

Fig 10.14   Block diagram configuration of trip computer control unit

Calibration

When the trip computer or any of the sensors have been replaced or in the event of incorrect functional displays, it is necessary to calibrate the system to ensure matching of components.

Vehicle condition monitoring

Vehicle condition monitoring (VCM) systems provided the driver with an indication of the operational state of various systems and functions that are the subject of legislation and/or are vital to the safety and operation of the vehicle. A VCM system generally monitors all functions automatically and constantly, and makes an active display of any malfunction.

The following systems/functions can be monitored:

- coolant level
- fluid level, clutch and brake fluid, screenwash water level
- engine oil level
- lights
- brake pad wear
- oil contamination
- engine operating conditions,

providing the driver with compliance with the law, safe driving, indication of potential costly faults and advising routine maintenance checks – the integration of service interval indicators inform the driver when the time has arrived for the next service, rather than being fixed by time or mileage.

Systems are available for monitoring single and multi-functions, with each monitoring channel comprising a sensor, electronic control unit and display. The principles of operation and design of each system varies according to the parameter being monitored and the operating environment. The construction and operation of the control unit, incorporating the input device, signal processing and the display drive circuitry, also varies with the application. Single channel systems (Fig 10.15) use standard integrated circuits, while the multi-channel systems are based on microprocessors (Fig 10.16). The display drivers use depend on the type of display technology; filament-bulb, VFD, LCD, or LED, and the display format (i.e. dot matrix, alphanumeric, bar graph or symbolic) and, in turn, these depend on the parameters being monitored.

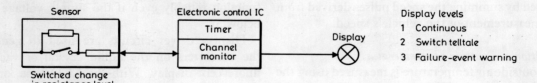

Fig 10.15   An individual monitoring channel comprises a sensing element, electronic circuit and illuminated warning display

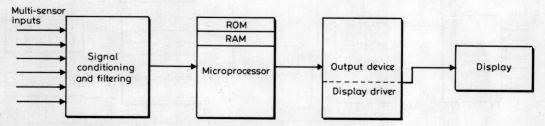

Fig 10.16   Multichannel microprocessor-based condition monitoring system

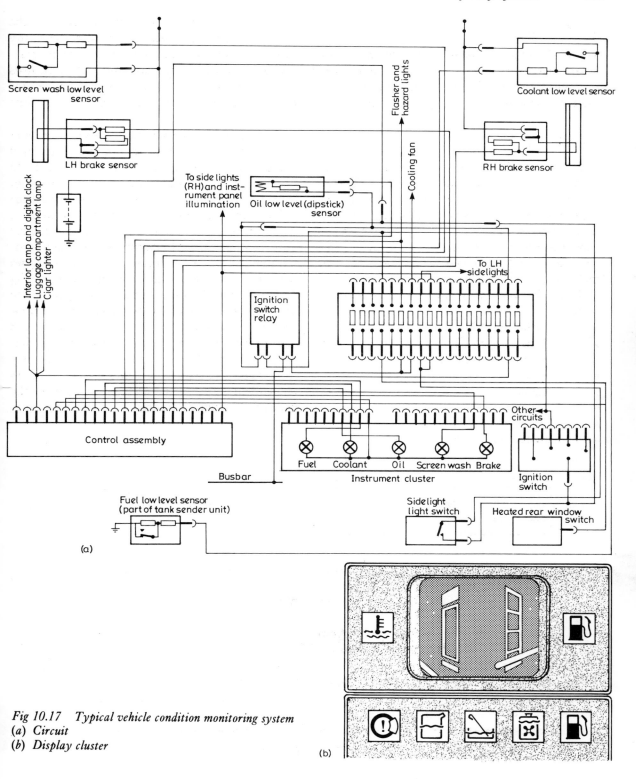

Fig 10.17 Typical vehicle condition monitoring system
(a) Circuit
(b) Display cluster

Typical system operation (Fig 10.17)

The sensors used to monitor each particular vehicle function do so by switching between high and low resistance values when preset functions limits are exceeded. The use of resistors avoids false readings due to a wiring fault (Fig 10.18). The two main types of sensors used: a float-switched magnet and reed switch sensor – used for low fluid level detection (for coolant, wash bottle,

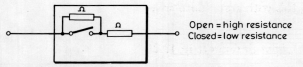

Open = high resistance
Closed = low resistance

(a) Resistance based sensor. Normally closed with short and/or open circuit detection. Normal logic 0; Failure logic 1

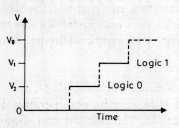

(b) Typical condition monitoring sensor signals

Fig 10.18   Principle of sensor switching action and signal levels
(a) *Resistance based sensor normally closed with short and/or open circuit detection. Normal-logic 0; failure-logic 1*
(b) *Typical condition monitoring sensor signals*

hydraulic fluid, fuel level) and a hot-wire resistance sensor (for oil level) and their operation in a VCM system have already been described in the chapter on sensors.

The control assembly integrated circuit provides timing signals and monitoring channels.

Timing signals automatically provide a check on the operation of all display lamps by generating a test signal of a predetermined duration (normally 5 seconds) each time the ignition is turned on which illuminates all the warning lamps. At the same time the status of each sensor assembly is

checked. If the status is within limits the display lamps will go out after the 5 seconds.

However, if an open circuit or earth fault is detected on any of the sensor supply leads, the electronic monitoring circuit causes the warning lamp of the affected channel to flash for a preset period (40 seconds) and then go out. This warning is repeated following each subsequent warning lamp test period until the sensor lead fault has been corrected.

If, on the other hand, a low level condition is present on a sensor, the appropriate warning lamp is illuminated continuously.

Following the initial start-up all sensors, with the exception of the oil sensor, are monitored continuously while the ignition is on and if a low level occurs at any time the corresponding warning is illuminated. The oil level is checked only once during each ignition on period: at the very beginning. This is because there is no point in constantly monitoring oil level: as soon as the engine turns oil is pumped out of the sump and a low-level would be sensed. Further, if the engine stands for less than about three minutes between running periods the oil does not have enough time to drain completely back to the sump – most VCM systems simply use the *previous* sensed level and display that unless more than three minutes has elapsed. Oil level sensing often has its own dedicated monitoring IC.

The coolant, fuel and screen wash sensors are interrogated for a continuous 8 seconds before a warning is displayed. This is to prevent lamp flicker due to fluid movement in the container. When the vehicle's side lights are on the warning lights are automatically dimmed – for night driving. One of the channels on the control assembly has a dual input and can be used for monitoring a system with two sensors but only one warning display (for example, a brake fluid level sensor and a brake pad wear sensor may be used to drive a single brake warning lamp).

The brake pad wear sensor is, in fact, a small wire loop, embedded in the brake pad at a depth of about 1.5 mm from minimum thickness of pad (Fig 10.19). Two resistors, of resistance 180 ohm

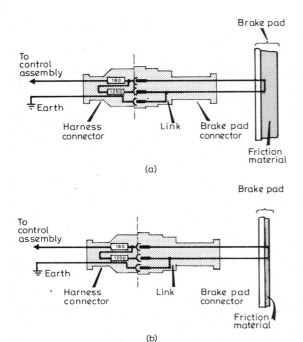

Fig 10.19   Brake pads sensor
(a) When brake pad is not worn
(b) When brake pad is worn

and 1200 ohm, are housed in the wiring harness connector to help differentiate between a disconnected sensor and a worn brake pad.

When the pad thickness is greater than 1.5 mm the resistance between the terminals is 180 ohm. When the pad is worn down, on the other hand, the wire loop becomes open circuit and the resist-

ance increases to 1380 ohm, activating the warning circuit.

The monitoring capacity of the control unit can be increased with the addition of a further two ICs dedicated to purely monitoring functions. These additional monitoring ICs are dependent upon the main assembly for the various timing signals which control the operating modes of warning lamps. Where a VCM system has or needs more than twelve monitoring channels, however, it is more economic and reliable to replace the discrete ICs with a microprocessor.

Light defects (Fig 10.20)

The monitoring of pertinent lights: stop lights; tail lights; number plate light; low beam etc, may be done by separate or combined monitoring units. Monitoring in these units is accomplished either with electromagnetically operated reed switches or with semiconductor devices (Fig 10.21).

Reed switch monitoring (Fig 10.21(a))
When the light circuits are operating the light's current, flowing through the coil winding of the monitoring unit, is sufficient to create an electromagnetic force to hold the normally closed reed. Switch contacts open, breaking the earth circuit of the monitor display lamp. If a light filament fails or an open circuit occurs in the wiring no current can flow through the coil wind-

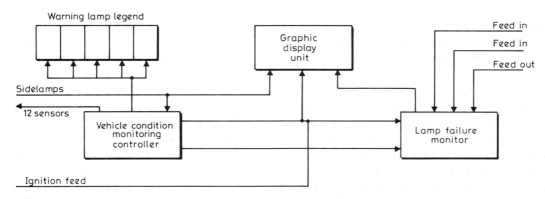

Fig 10.20   Condition monitoring system which includes lights failure detection

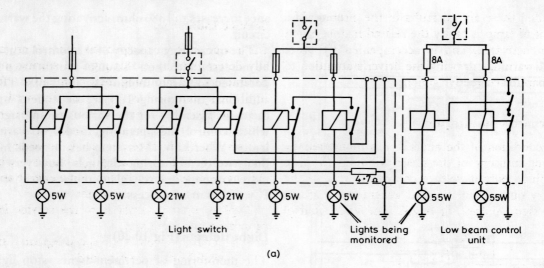

Light switch　　　Lights being monitored　　Low beam control unit

(a)

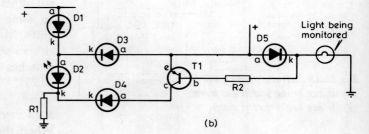

Fig 10.21　Light failure monitoring
(a) Reed switch
(b) Semiconductor

(b)

ing, closing the reed switch contacts, making the earth circuit of the monitor display lamp.

Semiconductor monitoring (Fig 10.21(b))
When the light circuits are operating, transistor T_1 is on, preventing LED D_2 from lighting up. With a failed light filament or broken wiring circuit, transistor T_1 is off and D_2 lights up.

VCM map displays

The vehicle map (Fig 10.22) is shaped like a car viewed from the top, and graphically displays the following information; door open; boot open; side lamps; dipped beam; mean beam; turn indicators; brake lamps; rear fog lamps; rear number plate lamp. The various map functions illuminate when their circuits are activated in different colours to the outline colour (yellow) when the ignition is switched on. Typical colours are:

- main beam and dipped beam　　blue
- side, tail and number plate　　white
- rear fog, brake　　red
- turn indicators　　green
- doors open　　red

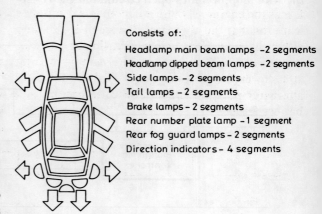

Consists of:

Headlamp main beam lamps – 2 segments
Headlamp dipped beam lamps – 2 segments
Side lamps – 2 segments
Tail lamps – 2 segments
Brake lamps – 2 segments
Rear number plate lamp – 1 segment
Rear fog guard lamps – 2 segments
Direction indicators – 4 segments

Fig 10.22　MAP display layout

provided there are no faults in the circuits. If a circuit or lamp is faulty the related map segment is not activated, and is accompanied by other VCM warnings drawing the driver's attention to the map for corrective action.

Alternator monitoring

The condition of the alternator is monitored by tapping into one of the phase windings to sense the phase output voltage comparing it with the battery output voltage, and generating a square wave signal pulse (Fig 10.23). The VCM control

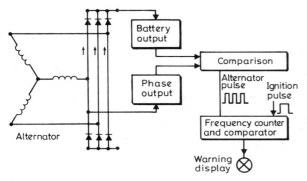

Fig 10.23   Alternator condition monitoring system

unit compares the frequency of this square wave with the frequency of ignition pulses. There should be a ratio of 7.5 alternator pulses for each ignition pulse, because the alternator is geared, through the pulley ratio, to revolve 7.5 times as fast as the engine. If there are more ignition pulses it means that the alternator drive belt is slipping; either through wear, incorrect tension or the rotor is starting to seize up, and the alternator is rotating at a slower than normal speed. If there are more alternator pulses this could be an indication of a battery fault.

Service indicator

Oil service or service inspection intervals are usually determined by evaluating and storing input parameters and summing their cumulative effects until the system decides a service is required.

In their simplest form service indicators take account only of vehicle mileage and time since the last service. The more advanced, however, also take account of the operating conditions to which the engine is subjected by including engine speed and temperature as input parameters.

Typical input parameters to the service indicator control system are:

- engine speed – all speeds greater than 4500 r/min are recorded
- engine temperature – each cold start is monitored and all temperatures below 50°C are recorded, as measured by the coolant temperature sensor
- time – the service due condition is always displayed after approximately 11–12 months from the date of resetting after the last service
- distance – derived from the vehicle speed sensor: The distance driven since the last service inspection.

Turning on the ignition causes the electronic display to indicate the instantaneous state until the next oil service or inspection (Fig 10.24). Initially the interval to the next service may be 12,000 units; this decreases at the rate of 1 unit per mile travelled, or at a faster rate if high engine speeds or low temperature starts occur. When more than about 1200 units remain, the interval left until a service is due is displayed in green. Below 1200 yellow or orange segments display the interval. When the service interval has been exhausted red segments and a 'service due' symbol is displayed.

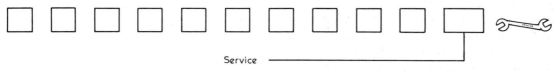

Fig 10.24   Typical service interval illuminating segments

The display is reset to full scale after the vehicle has been serviced. To ensure correct operation of the service interval gauge (SIG) the calendar must always be set properly before the SIG is reset, and after each battery disconnection. Some SIGs employ the use of buffer batteries to ensure having the same display as before, after removing the instrument panel or disconnecting the car battery.

Ensure that these buffer batteries are fully charged before disconnecting. The resetting procedure must follow the manufacturer's instructions in order to cancel the memory.

Voice synthesis

The voice synthesiser is an electronic device which

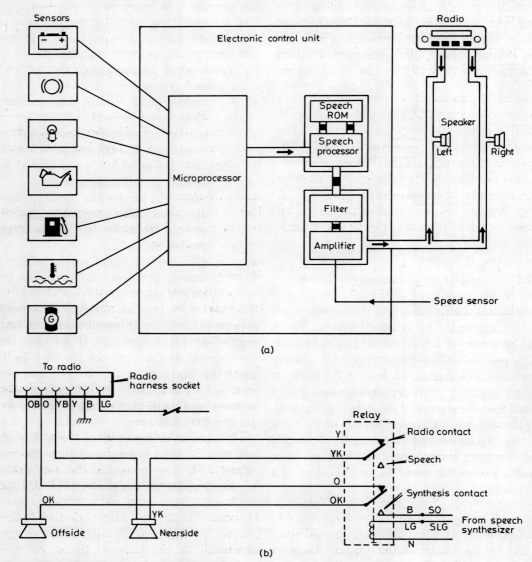

(a)

(b)

Fig 10.25   Typical voice synthesiser VCM system
(a) Block diagram
(b) Circuit to allow voice message to cut-off audio output

uses a synthesised voice to warn the driver of information or conditions which might not otherwise be noticed. Driving a vehicle imposes a very heavy visual load on the driver. The driver's hearing is, however, less heavily involved and can be used as an information channel to support visual displays in conveying warnings to the driver of critical vehicle operating conditions and/or trip computer information. This results in improved safety as the driver is free to concentrate on observation of the traffic and road conditions, and better driver information through the use of verbal messages accompanied by advice.

The voice synthesiser comprises an electronic control unit fed by some 20 sensors (Fig 10.25) and broadcasts its messages through either a separate loudspeaker or the audio equipment fitted to the vehicle. If the latter, the voice synthesiser message takes precedence over the audio output.

Messages can be synthesised in a number of ways. A common way is to record, digitally, each possible human voice sound (known as a phoneme) in ROM memory (Fig 10.26). Repro-

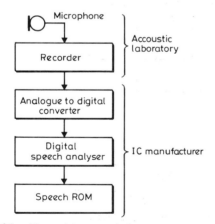

Fig 10.26   Memorising speech data

duction of a message is now possible by addressing in turn each phoneme required to make up the message, converting them all back to analogue form, filtering to smooth out the stepped changes, and finally amplifying (Fig 10.27). Special speech-processor microprocessors and speech memories are used.

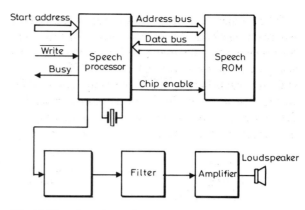

Fig 10.27   Speech synthesis system

The following functions are usually monitored by voice synthesis VCM systems, with messages coming in three categories: 1 attention alerts; 2 warnings; 3 information.

Attention alerts
Fall in oil pressure, engine overheating, charging system failure, braking circuit failure (repeated every few seconds).

Warnings
Low coolant level, low fuel level, stop light defective, brake pads warning, side light failure, low oil level (once after ignition is turned on, or every 10 minutes).

Information
Door not closed, light left on, handbrake not released, all functions working normally, or service required (once only).

The messages are also listed in order of broadcast priority. The low priority messages can be restricted from use, but not the high priorities. All phrases stored in the speech ROM can be checked out by pressing the appropriate test keys. To avoid unnecessary interruption while driving, defects are announced only after a repeated monitoring of the sensors. If the driver is to be informed, a gong-type sound precedes the announcement. Important warnings begin with words such as: attention; alert; or warning.

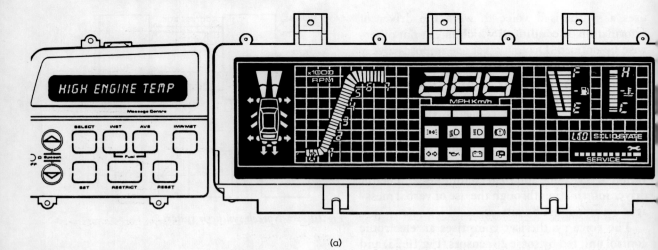

(a)

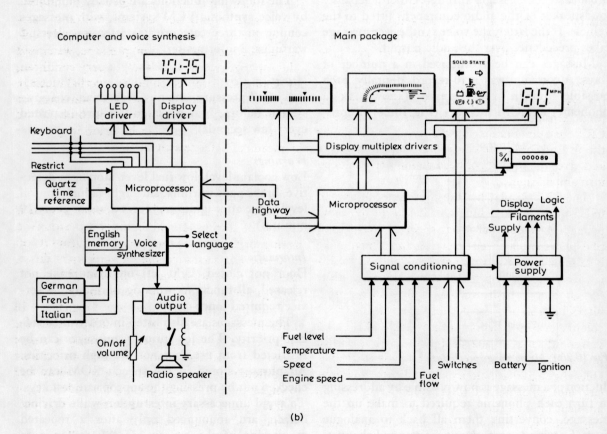

(b)

Fig 10.28   A typical integrated driver information management system
(a) Display layout
(b) Circuit details

Driver information management

Experience in vehicle electronics and advanced display technologies is leading to the implementation of total information systems for the automobile. The first step is the addition of a trip computer to a vehicle's VCM system, common in many of today's top-of-the-range models. Integrating all driver information functions into a single display is the next step. Indeed, a number of examples of integrated systems already exist (Fig 10.28).

The integrated driver information centre uses microprocessor-based control systems to selectively manage what the instrument panel displays. It can also monitor conditions and give trip information. Information can be backed up and provided in speech form, and display of information can be either VFD, LCD or cathode ray tube (CRT).

Generally, the use of VFD or LCD means that the style of the display and the symbols etc are predetermined and cannot be altered. The use of CRT instrumentation, on the other hand, allows the use of computer controlled graphic displays and gives the benefits of both digital and analogue instrumentation.

The CRT display has the appearance of a small television tube, and indeed is based on the same principles except that it has specially formulated phosphors and a special electron gun which make it suitable for use in automobiles. Data and graphics are presented on the screen in a sharp, clear format that is easily readable. When used with filters information can be displayed in up to six colours. A block diagram of a typical CRT-based driver information management centre is shown in Fig 10.29. The centre monitors some 30 variables, has a 100K memory, and adjusts the intensity of the displayed information according to ambient light. Although only one CRT is shown, the centre can be used with more (some vehicle manufacturers are using the centre with three, 120 mm CRTs) to display more information.

A whole mass of information can be displayed. Typically, vehicle speed and engine rev/min are

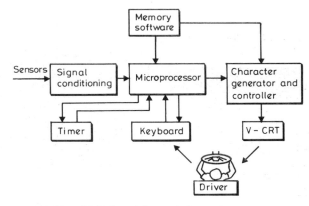

Fig 10.29   CRT-based driver information management centre block diagram

shown by climbing streams of green light, and bar graphs give information on fuel level and water temperature. There are also appropriately coloured warning symbols on oil pressure, water and oil temperature, low fuel level, battery condition, icy conditions, supplemented by a verbal message from a voice synthesiser. Symbolic warnings for seat belts, heated rear window and bulb failure are provided, but these can be made inoperative by means of a delete switch.

Electronic controlled power seats

In this application the microprocessor system is capable of storing four different seat positions in its memory, so that at the touch of a button it will move the seat backward and forward, up or down, back rest inclination and headrest height, reproducing exactly the position stored in memory.

The programmable memory registers 10 different combinations of seat adjustments for each of the positions stored, enabling a single driver to code in a number of positions suitable for different types of driving, eg motorway and town, or each of several drivers can code in their own favourite position. In addition, the seat position can be changed manually.

Fig 10.30 shows the system in detail. Sensors are attached to the electric motor actuators which control seat movement and adjustment. With each revolution of actuator gear the corresponding

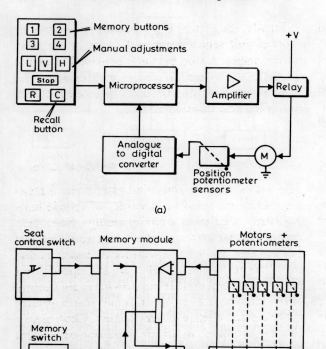

(a)

(b)

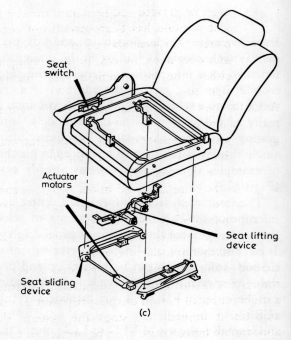

(c)

Fig 10.30 *Programmable power-seat positioning system*
(a) *Functional control diagram*
(b) *Block wiring diagram*
(c) *Motors and actuating mechanism*

sensor sends position information to the micro-processor, via an analogue-to-digital converter. The microprocessor compares the actual position with the position requested by the driver, adjusting the seat accordingly until the difference between is zero. The position motors are driven by signals from the output stage which operate the relays connecting the motors to the battery. The motors are arranged in two groups for seat positioning:

• group 1 – backward, forward, front cushion height and the head restraint
• group 2 – backrest inclination and rear cushion height.

When one of the manual adjustment buttons is pressed the control unit directly activates the appropriate relay connecting battery voltage to the motor, causing the seat to move position for as long as the button is depressed. During this action sensor signals are monitored by the micro-

processor, and stored in RAM as a digital code if the position memory key is then pressed.

If a position recall button is pressed the micro-processor assigns the corresponding seat position codes to the program command and then compares these codes one after the other to the corresponding sensor signals. If they are not the same, the motors are driven in their appropriate directions, until all match exactly. The seat will then be in the correct position as memorised.

Two programs are provided to recall the four stored seat positions:

1   recalling a memorised seat position automatically: by pressing the pertinent recall push button. The ignition switch must be at position 1 (battery auxiliary) or 2 (ignition on) and the engine not running

2   recalling a memorised seat position with the engine running and vehicle speeds below 5 mph: the position recall button

must be pressed and held until the stored seat position has been carried out completely. At speeds above 5 mph the control unit does not allow seat positioning using either the programmable or manual switches.

A LED gives a visual indication of the control action taking place:

- storage of seat position when the memory button is being pressed – the LED flashes at a high frequency
- seat being adjusted under program control – LED on continuously until the seat position has been reached
- seat reaches stored position – LED flashes at a slow frequency.

Certain safety precautions are provided to protect the system against incorrect operation. Operating a different recall button during programmed seat adjustment immediately stops the system: the appropriate button must then be pressed to complete seat adjustment. Manual control always takes precedence over programmed control.

Finally, the system is protected against open or short circuit sensor leads and faults in the relay output stages. A stop button is provided to switch off the entire system in case of malfunction. The stop button can also be used to interrupt each unwanted seat position action.

Electronic control of interior temperatures

The use of micro–electronic heater control techniques has increased the accuracy of vehicle temperature regulation, consequently improving driver and passenger comfort. Electronic control can compensate for temperature fluctuations due to different engine speeds, driving speeds and outside temperatures. It can provide rapid heating of the interior after a cold start and reacts quickly to the desired change in temperature. Control may also be extended to an air conditioning system which both cools the air and removes moisture from it, so maintaining an even more constant interior environment – particularly in hot weather.

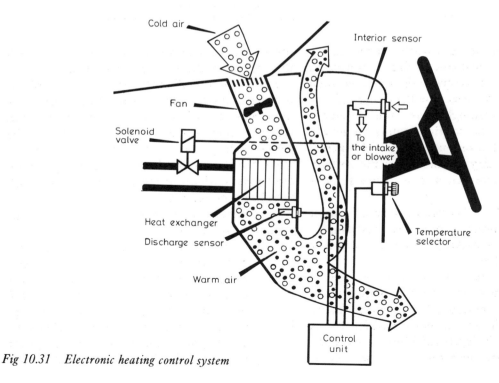

Fig 10.31   Electronic heating control system

Heater control

Vehicle heating systems regulate the interior temperature simply by changing the amount of hot water passing through a heater radiator (heat exchanger). A control valve regulates the flow rate of the hot water. An electronic automatic heater system is shown in Fig 10.31 and comprises sensors, actuators, control unit and a temperature selection potentiometer.

Temperature sensors

Quality of control depends mainly upon the position and response time of the temperature sensors. Two NTC thermistors are used: one to measure the interior temperature (located so that air from the vehicle interior is continually being forced over the sensor to ensure a rapid response); the other to monitor the temperature of the air being discharged from the heat exchanger into the interior (located as close to the discharge vent of the exchanger as possible). The signals from these two sensors are fed to the control unit for comparison with the desired temperature.

The desired interior temperature is selected by rotation of a potentiometer, which incorporates a limit switch for continuous heat and an off switch for no heat (i.e. cool air).

Control unit

Fig 10.32 shows a block diagram of the system, illustrating the control unit in detail. The two temperature sensor signals are evaluated with the desired temperature signal, and are then compared with a reference voltage provided by the sawtooth voltage generator. The electrical pulses obtained by this comparison are amplified in the driver circuit to operate the power output transistor. The power transistor earths the regulated voltage supplied to the solenoid valve.

Actuator

The hot water solenoid valve actuator (Fig 10.33)

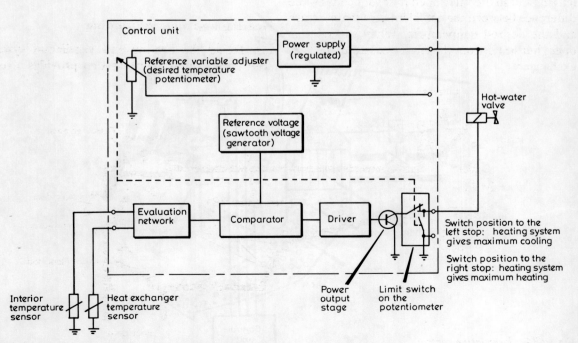

Fig 10.32   Electronic control unit for automatic heater

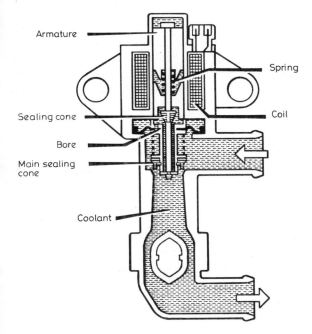

Armature

Spring

Sealing cone

Coil

Bore

Main sealing cone

Coolant

Fig 10.33   Hot water solenoid valve actuator

Ventilation control

Two additional functions are adjusted in the ventilation system:

1   air flow
2   air distribution.

Potentiometers are used to signal the driver's desire for air flow rate and distribution to the control unit. By means of an electronic pulse generator, whose output frequency is proportional to the air flow rate potentiometer's position, the rotational speed of the fan motor can be continuously varied. DC motor actuators, or solenoid operated pneumatic actuators, are used to adjust the position of air flaps for air distribution (Fig. 10.34).

Pushing the defrost button instructs the control unit to adjust the heating system for maximum heat, and to direct the whole air flow to the windscreen with the blower at maximum speed.

Pressing the ambient air button interrupts the supply of fresh air from outside the vehicle, while heating and blowing continue to function as requested by the driver.

Heating and air conditioning

Interfacing the heating and ventilation system with an air conditioning system provides a total

is operated by pulses from the control unit. Pulse length (and so the valve open time) depends on the difference between the actual interior temperature and the desired temperature. When the valve is open, hot water from the engine passes to the heat exchanger.

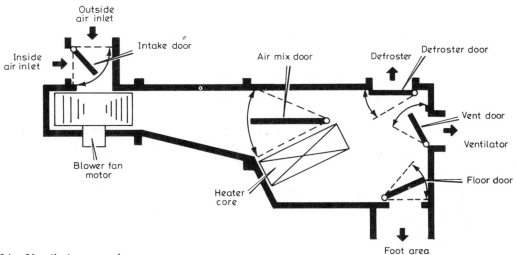

Outside air inlet

Inside air inlet

Intake door

Air mix door

Defroster

Defroster door

Vent door

Ventilator

Floor door

Blower fan motor

Heater core

Foot area

Fig 10.34   Ventilation control

system that will accurately maintain a desired interior temperature level, whatever the environmental conditions. In effect, cooling as well as heating is controlled.

Air conditioning systems operate on the same principle as domestic refrigerators. A refrigerant coolant gas is alternately compressed and expanded (Fig 10.35). The gas is first compressed

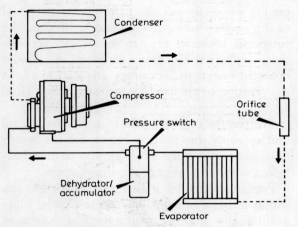

Fig 10.35   Refrigeration process as used in air conditioning systems

by a pump (the compressor) and cooled in a condensor, where it liquefies. It is then passed into an evaporator where it expands and boils, absorbing heat from the surroundings – the evaporator is thus cooler than the environment – and back to the compressor.

By blowing air across the evaporator the vehicle interior can thus be made cooler than the external temperature – something which an ordinary heater and ventilation system cannot do.

Vehicle interior temperature sensors are installed at head and foot height. An exterior sensor is mounted at the front of the vehicle to monitor the ambient air temperature, while the amount of sunlight is monitored from a solar sensor attached to the outside surface of the vehicle body (Fig 10.36(a)).

When starting the engine in cold weather the system immediately operates in the defrost mode until the coolant temperature rises to a preset

level, thereby preventing 'fogging' on the windscreen. As the engine coolant temperature rises high enough for the heater to be used, the outlet flaps are automatically actuated, and the control unit maintains temperature of the desired level.

When defrost is switched on, manually, the air flow is automatically set to maximum by pulsing the blower. This can, however, be overridden and switched to minimum, manually. Signal lamps indicate the mode of heating and ventilation being used.

Air conditioner (A/C) systems generally have three main switches, one to turn the A/C on and off, a fan switch to turn the blower on and off and the temperature select switch. When the A/C is switched on the control unit maintains the desired temperature by engaging or disengaging an electromagnetic clutch in the compressor. When engaged the refrigerant is pumped around the circuit to maintain the coolness of the interior. The compressor clutch is automatically disengaged when the outside temperature is below 0°C. Air flow direction flaps are also automatically controlled (Fig 10.36(b)).

Some A/C systems have a feature which advances the vehicle's ignition timing when the A/C automatic mode is selected. This improves engine torque and compensates for the increased load on the engine due to the A/C. If switched to economy mode, interior cooling is carried out by simple ventilation using the outside air only (or interior air if the recirculation switch is used) and the compressor is switched off.

Safety circuits

A refrigerant leak warning device is built into the A/C system. Its purpose is to prevent damage due to continued operation when there is a shortage of refrigerant, and also to indicate when to replenish the refrigerant. The sensor for the leak warning system (Fig 13.37) is generally located in the pressure switch.

If there is insufficient refrigerant, then what refrigerant is inside the evaporator vaporises much more quickly, with a corresponding increase in temperature and pressure of the refrigerant at the

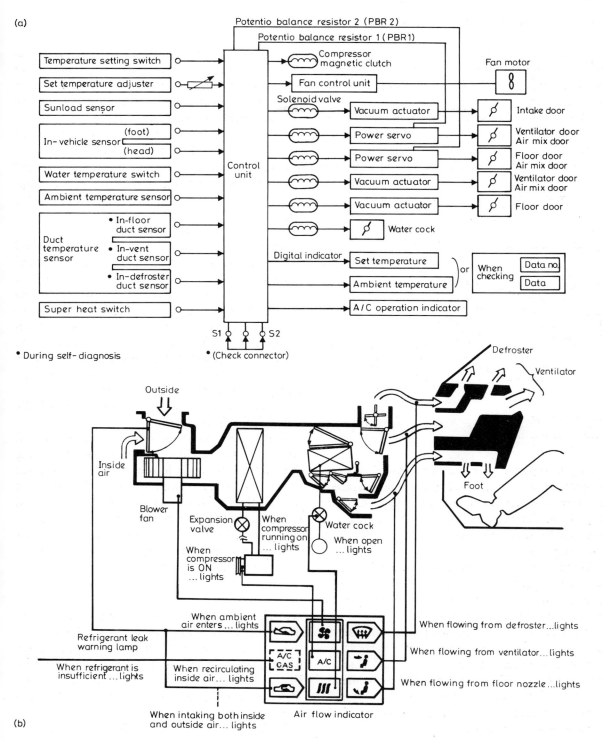

Fig 10.36 Typical electronically controlled air conditioner
(a) Control system block diagram
(b) Schematic layout of input switched and controlled actuators

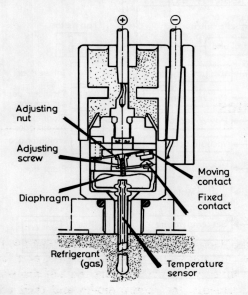

Fig 10.37   Temperature and pressure sensor used in low refrigerant warning system of an air conditioner

outlet. Whenever the coolant temperature exceeds 40–45°C a time delay circuit is activated. If activated for more than 60 seconds the time delay turns on a warning light. This delay prevents incorrect signals being displayed as would occur, say, during rapid acceleration when there is a corresponding rapid rise in refrigerant temperature. A steady state increase in temperature only

occurs, however, when the amount of refrigerant is low.

Self diagnosis

A self diagnosis mode is typically provided to locate simple faults in the input and output circuits. When switched to diagnostic mode the temperature display is used to indicate the sensor and circuit being checked, and a coded message of their conditions (Table 10.1). The temperature set buttons are used to switch to the input circuits to be checked.

The diagnostic mode checks the operation of the output circuits by sequentially operating the six actuators; moving them between stoke ends or changing all positions. Satisfactory operation can be determined by applying a hand to the outlet door, observing the air flow indicator, listening and looking at the operation, or by measuring the applied voltage.

New developments

Air conditioning compressors which automatically vary displacement to match cooling demands are now being fitted to new vehicles. No on–off cycling of a magnetic clutch is necessary in such compressors and fewer circuit variations are required for cutting out the compressor load to match combinations of operating conditions – giving up to 2 mpg improvement in fuel economy.

Table 10.1   Self-diagnosis fault display code and associated component part.

Display no.	Item of input signal	Parts name
0	Temperature of inside air temperature sensor (foot)	In-vehicle sensor (foot)
1	Temperature of in-vehicle sensor (head)	In-vehicle sensor (head)
2	Temperature of floor outlet	Floor duct temperature sensor
3	Temperature of ventilator outlet	Ventilator duct temperature sensor
4	Temperature of defroster outlet	Defroster duct temperature sensor
5	Water temperature SW display ON-OFF	Water temperature SW
6	Sunload	Sunload sensor
7	Width of objective temperature	Set temperature adjuster
8	Position of A/M door 2	PBR 2
9	Position of A/M door 1	PBR 1
10–15	No meaning	No meaning

11

On–board diagnostic techniques

The complexity of many electronic control systems requires that self-diagnosis of system failures be included in the software program. Basically the diagnostic routine alerts the driver, through a warning indicator, that a failure has occurred and service is required. The diagnostic system can also be an aid to the service technician in pinpointing the problem area. This is useful because fault-finding in microprocessor-based systems is different to that in analogue and other digital logic circuits, and a number of problems are decidedly peculiar to microprocessor-based systems:

1   operation depends on the flow of a sequence of instructions. If a single program bit or byte is in error the whole system may lock out – noise and bad memory bits are common sources of error. These failures are difficult to pinpoint because the whole system may operate incorrectly.

2   signals within the system can be in excess of 5 MHz, which makes it difficult to obtain meaningful results

3   use of bus structures makes it possible to connect many complex devices to a common line – any error signals are thus routed to all devices

4   the faults can either be software or hardware induced, though if the system has been in use for some time the fault is more likely to be due to a hardware component failure.

Self diagnostics is not without its own peculiar problems and could itself be a source of a fault. As a first step in establishing the self diagnostic requirements, the failure modes and their effect on the vehicle must be analysed:

● disabling – a failure which prevents operation of the vehicle

● detectable degradation – a failure that results in poor vehicle performance

● undetectable degradation – a failure which causes the system to operate outside the normal parameters, but is not discernible

● inconsequential – a failure which has no effect on performance under normal conditions but could result in poor performance under a multiple failure situation.

Self-test diagnostic software, though requiring additional memory, provides a flexible and low cost solution to fault-finding. Most systems, however, still use a degree of hardware to minimise the functions which would disable the system if software problems occur. Typical fail-safe hardware solutions are found in electronic fuel and ignition systems, to maintain operation (albeit to a limited degree) when failure occurs in the microprocessor due to software problems.

In general, self-test diagnostic routines:

1   inform the driver a fault has occurred, by illuminating an indicator.

2   store a specific code for the fault in non-

volatile memory for later read-out by the service technician, as a fault location aid.

3   maintain system operation and bypass the faulty element by either substituting a fixed value for the failed element (e.g. if the temperature sensor system fails a fixed temperature is used) or by placing the control function units in normal operating state and thus disabling the faulty sub-system (e.g. if the oxygen sensor fails the closed-loop fuel control is disabled).

In most systems value substitution is usually made to maintain the basic vehicle functions. Function disablement is only used to prevent abnormal operating conditions.

Transient and intermittent faults are a significant problem for on-board fault diagnosis: as they are usually very difficult to trace, particularly when relying on the driver to describe the symptoms. The memory which would be required to record *all* transient faults and their characteristics would be huge and thus very expensive, therefore only limited facilities for this are provided:

●   all major faults are recorded in memory
●   self diagnostic test failures are recorded only if detected over a number of specific tests
●   all short duration transients are ignored
●   fault indication is only used for active faults
●   memory is cleared if no additional faults are detected within a number of specified cycles.

Obviously, the diagnostic software must distinguish between a fault condition and normal operation. This is done by establishing a precise set of operating conditions.

Service diagnostic techniques

Most on-board systems have to be switched to diagnostic mode to enable the service technician to read out the faults logged by the self-diagnostic routine. Read-out is by flashing the stored error codes via the fault indicator display, or (where off-board computer interfaces are used) by presenting the error codes numerically. Using the fault code documentation the fault can then be isolated to a specific element.

Additionally, discrete input and output tests can be initiated by the service technician which cause the input to be activated in a prescribed sequence. An indication is provided for each correct input. In the output test mode output signals are generally cycled on and off to check the proper operation of the actuators.

In vehicles with digital displays diagnostic routines are often provided to evaluate the sensor subsystems from transducer through the control unit itself. Certain performance data such as spark advance, fuel delivery, number of engine starts etc, since last recorded fault may be available, also, for display.

Self-test diagnostics are not usually provided for system failures where it is not possible to establish test conditions due to insufficient data, and for which it would be impractical to collect the data. These tests, though, are usually covered by the service technician's input and output tests.

Index